Let's Make Dice, Game Tokens, and Tiles!

How to Play

Cut out the dice and game tokens along the lines and assemble with glue. Cut out the tiles along the lines. You will use these pieces to play a game in several activities.

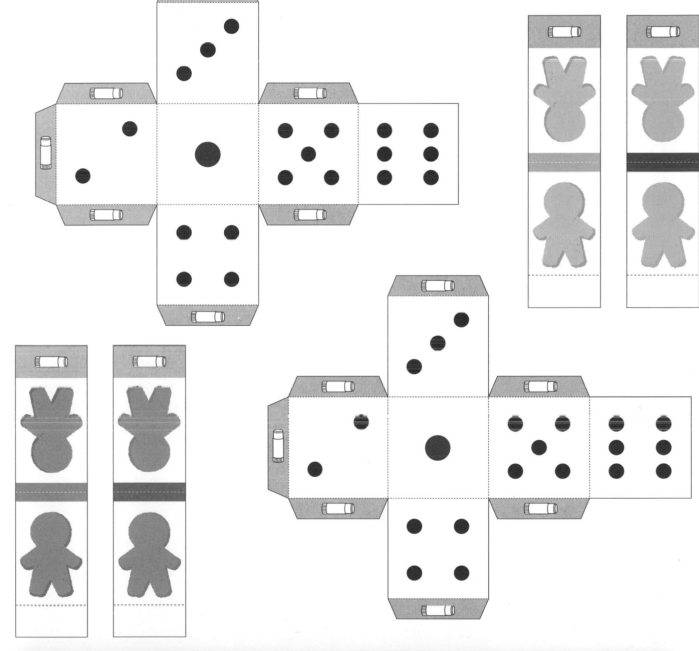

Everyday Math
Addition & Subtraction

Table of Contents

KUMON

Draw a line from 1 to 30 in order while saying each number aloud.

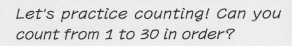

Let's practice counting! Can you count from 1 to 30 in order?

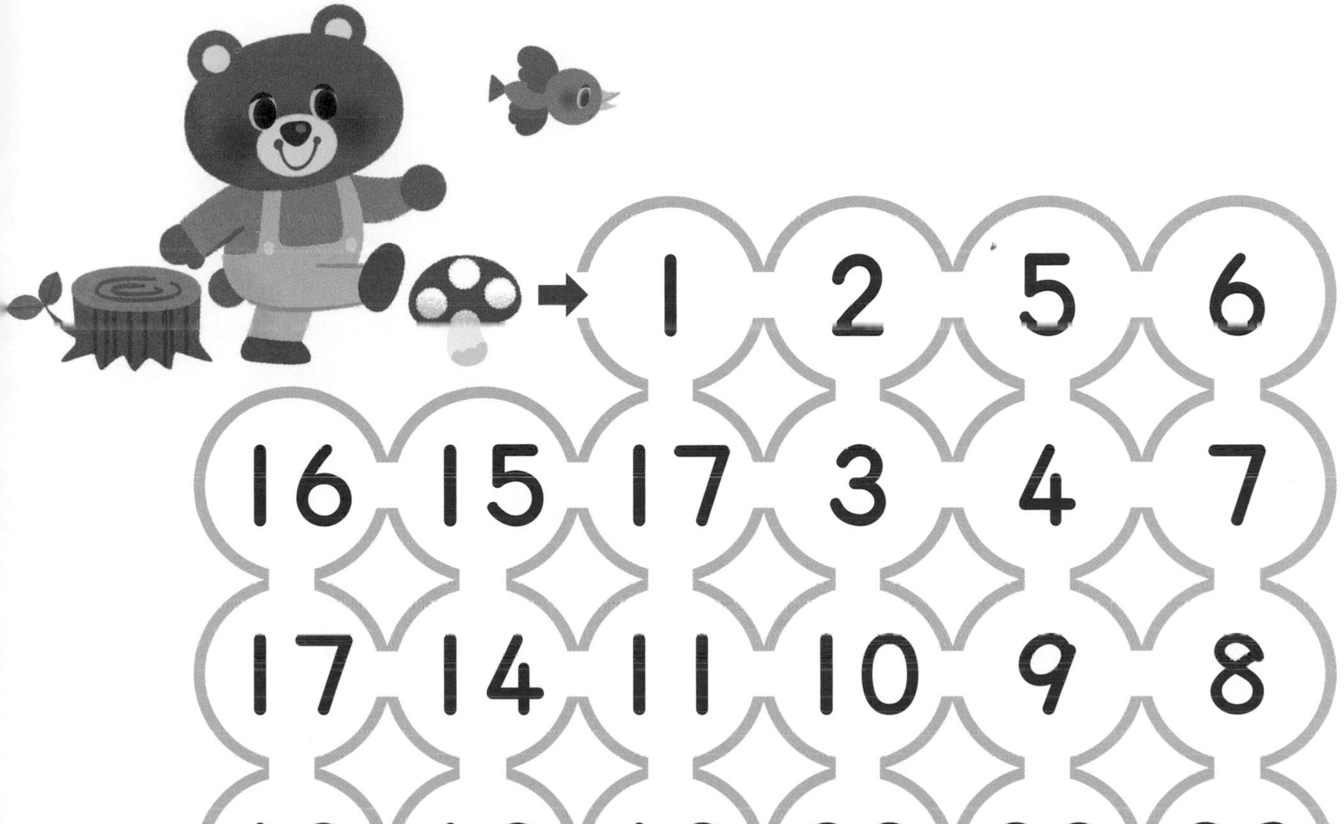

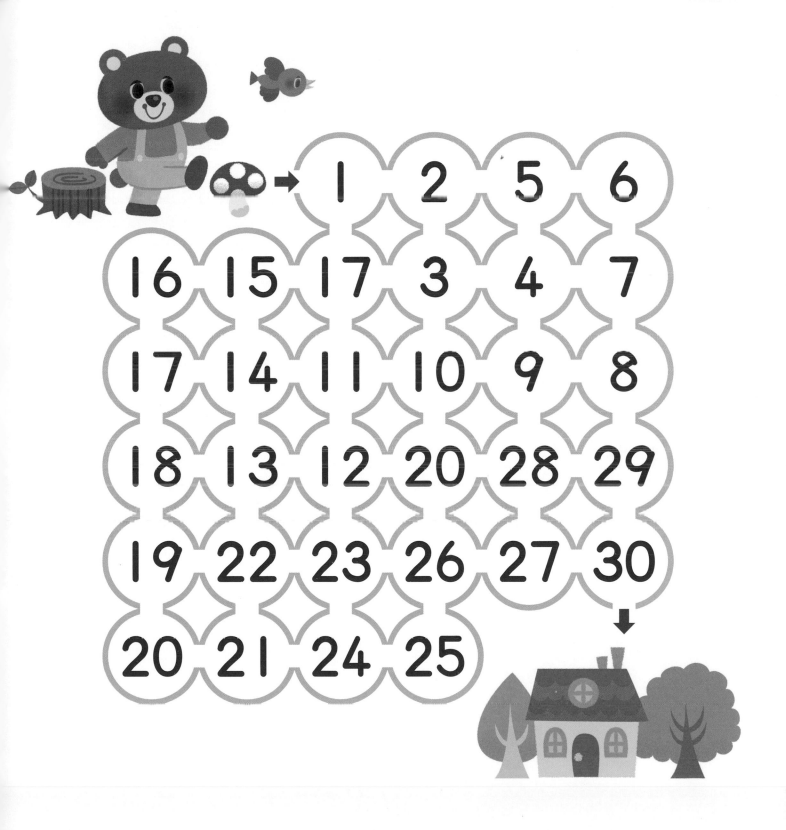

2 Place a check mark ( ) under the correct one.

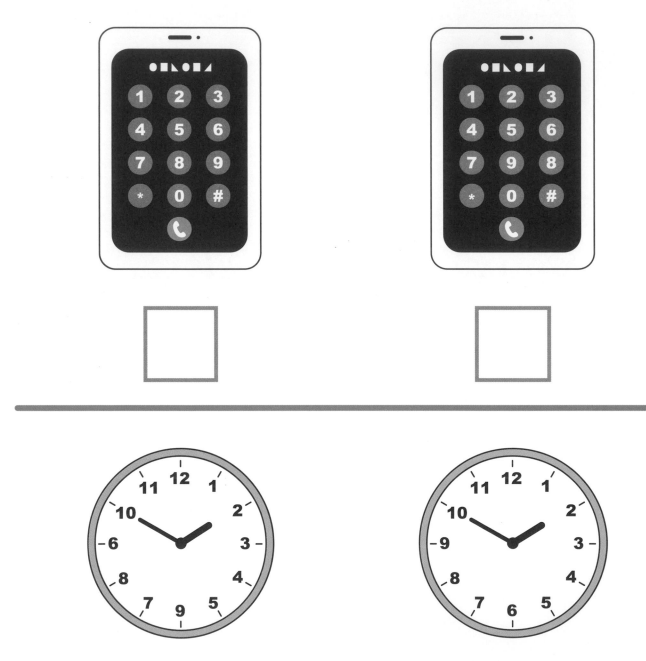

If you look closely, some of the numbers are out of order.

Numbers 1–30

1	2	3	4	5
6	7	8	9	10
11	12	23	14	15
16	17	18	19	20
21	22	13	24	25
26	27	28	29	30

Numbers 1–30

1	2	3	4	5
6	7	8	9	10
11	12	13	14	15
16	17	18	19	20
21	22	23	24	25
26	27	28	29	30

April 2024

Sunday	Monday	Tuesday	Wednesday	Thursday	Friday	Saturday
	1	2	3	4	5	6
7	8	9	10	11	12	13
14	15	16	17	18	19	20
21	22	23	24	25	26	27
28	29	30				

April 2024

Sunday	Monday	Tuesday	Wednesday	Thursday	Friday	Saturday
	1	2	3	4	5	6
7	8	9	10	11	12	13
14	15	16	17	18	19	20
21	23	22	24	25	26	27
28	29	30				

3

Draw a line to match the same number of objects.

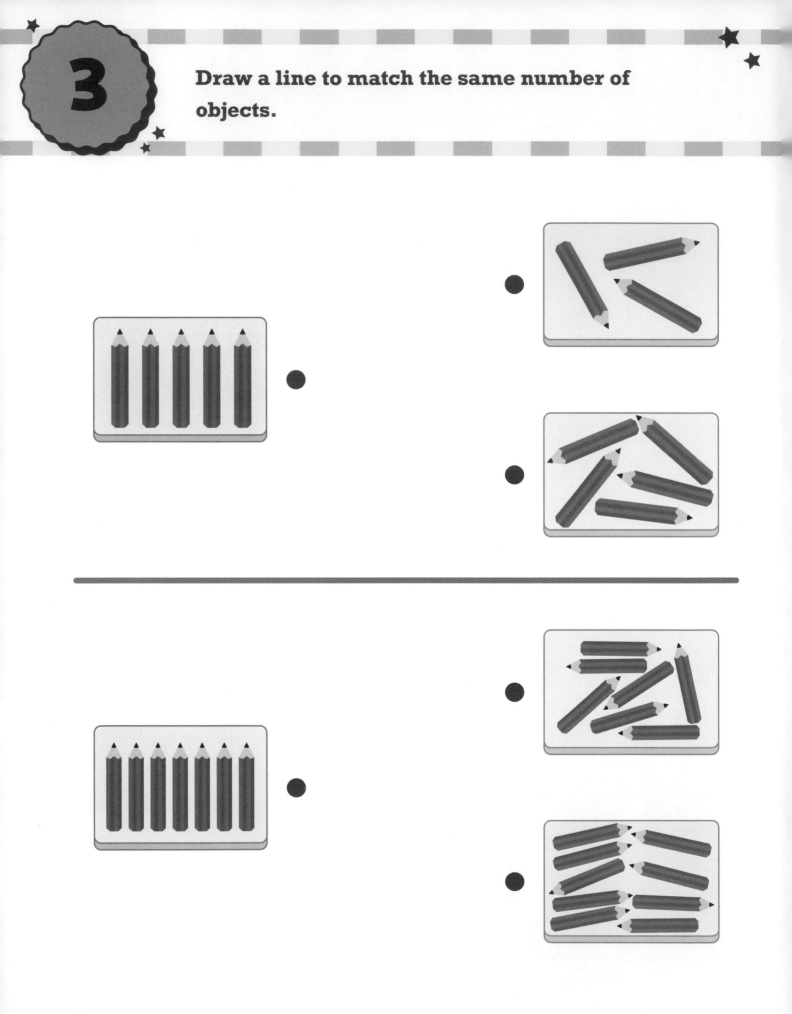

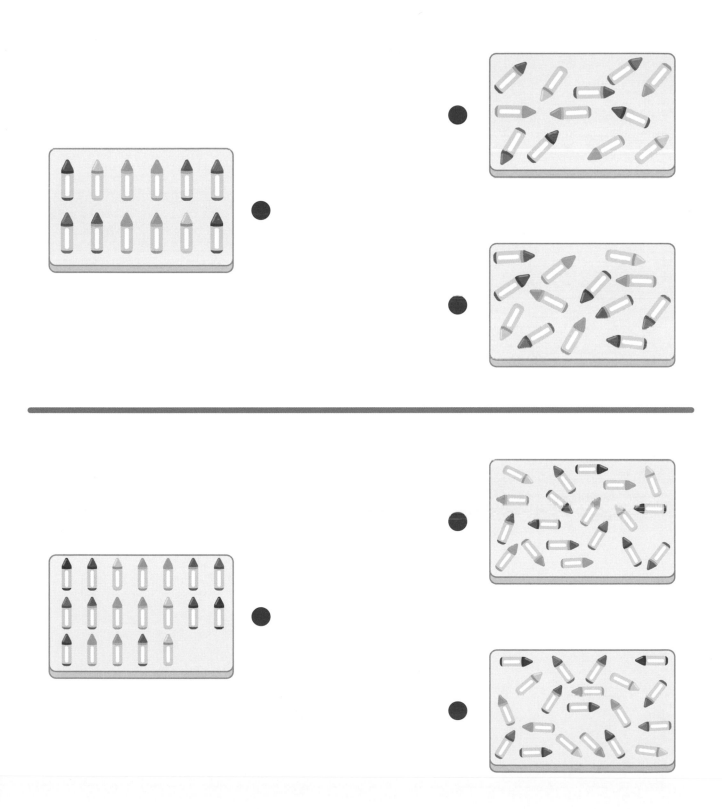

9

4

Place a check mark (✓) for correct statements and an "✗" for incorrect statements.

There are 8 butterflies.

There are 23 ants.

10

There are more ants than butterflies.

There are more butterflies than bees.

Draw a line to the correct answer.

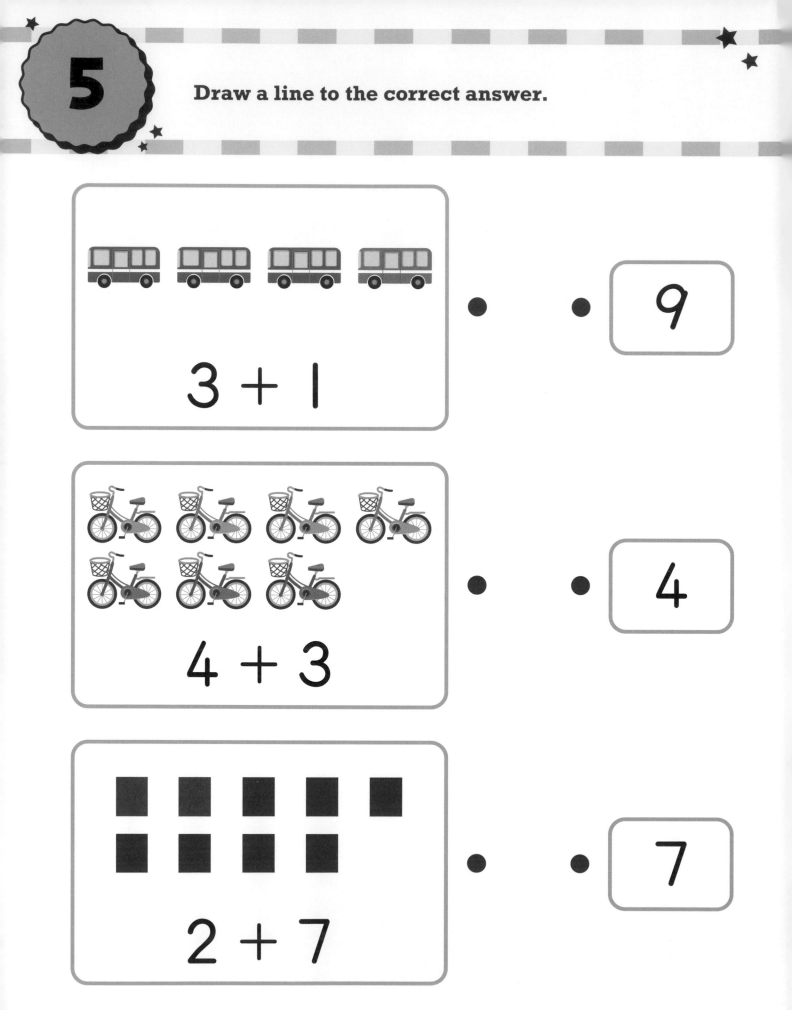

3 + 1

9

4 + 3

4

2 + 7

7

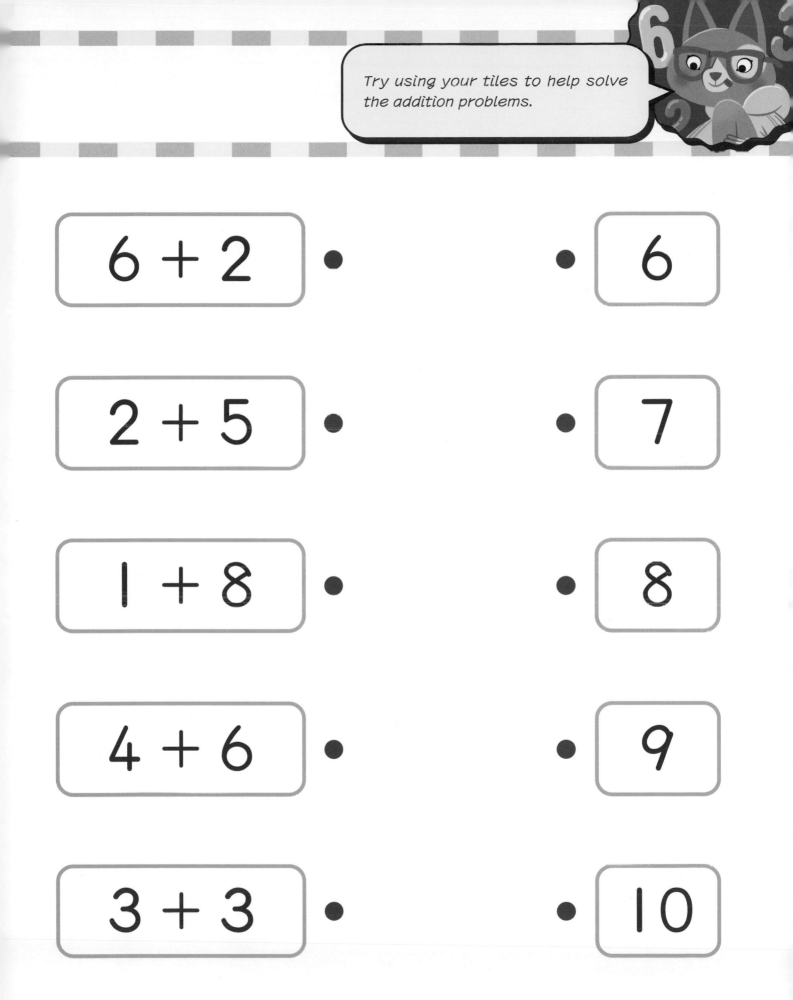

6 + 2 • • 6

2 + 5 • • 7

1 + 8 • • 8

4 + 6 • • 9

3 + 3 • • 10

6 Place a check mark (✔) for correct statements and an "✗" for incorrect statements.

There are a total of 5 lions and bears.

There are a total of 7 lions and giraffes.

14

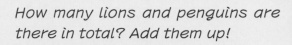

How many lions and penguins are there in total? Add them up!

There are a total of 7 bears and giraffes.

There are a total of 9 giraffes and penguins.

How much will each basket of pastries cost?
Write the number in the box.

$5

$3

$4

$2

That will be [7] dollars.

That will be [ ] dollars.

All of the pastries look delicious. Which one would you buy?

$7

$6

$4

$3

That will be ⬚ dollars.

That will be ⬚ dollars.

Which picture completes the scene? Place a check mark (✓) under the correct one.

( )

( )

How many cookies do the two children want to eat in total? Let's add them up.

I'll put 4 cookies on a plate.

( )

I'll put 8 cookies on a plate.

( )

Roll the dice and write the sum of the numbers.

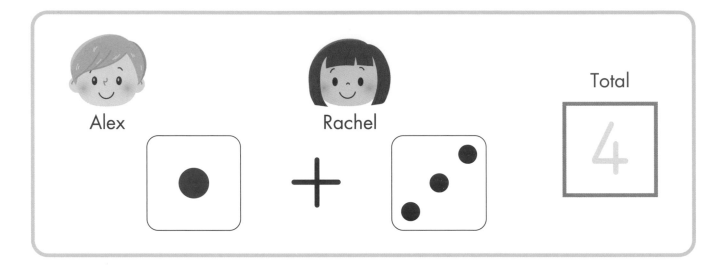

Alex + Rachel Total 4

Fred + Claire Total

Noah + Natalie Total

Try rolling the dice yourself! Use the dice you made, and record the number in the box that says, "You."

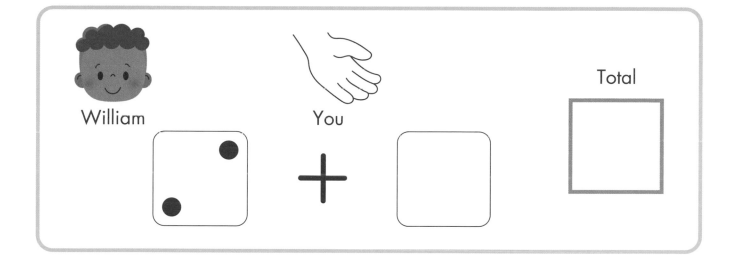

William
You
Total

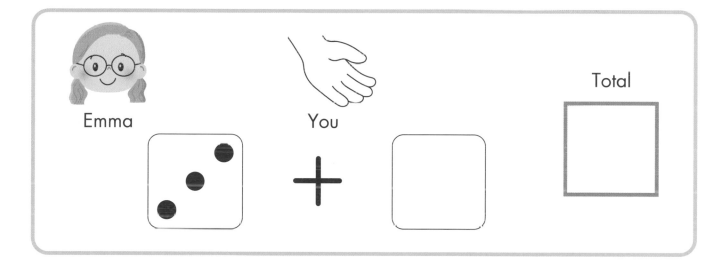

Emma
You
Total

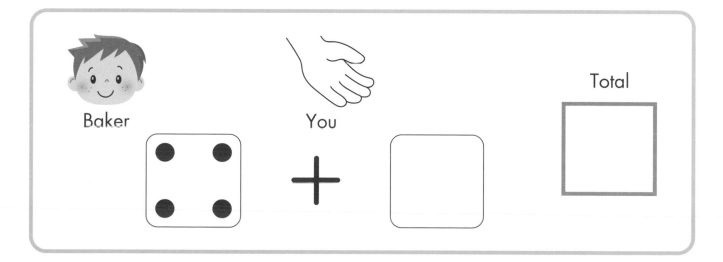

Baker
You
Total

Draw a line to the correct answer.

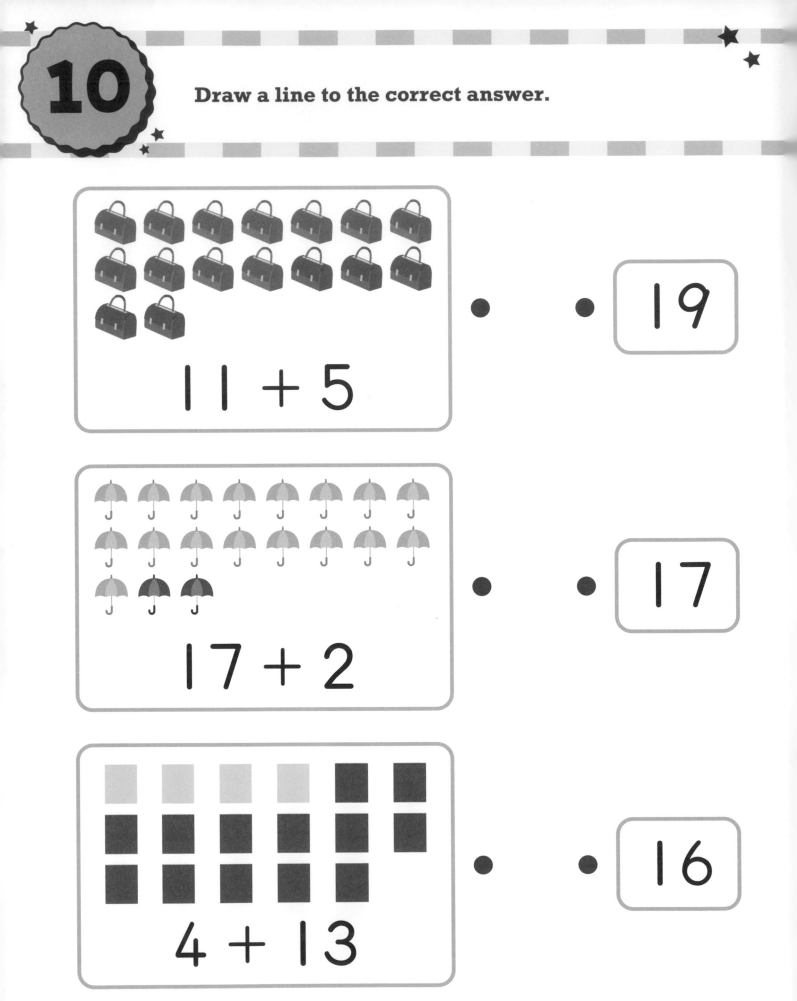

11 + 5

19

17 + 2

17

4 + 13

16

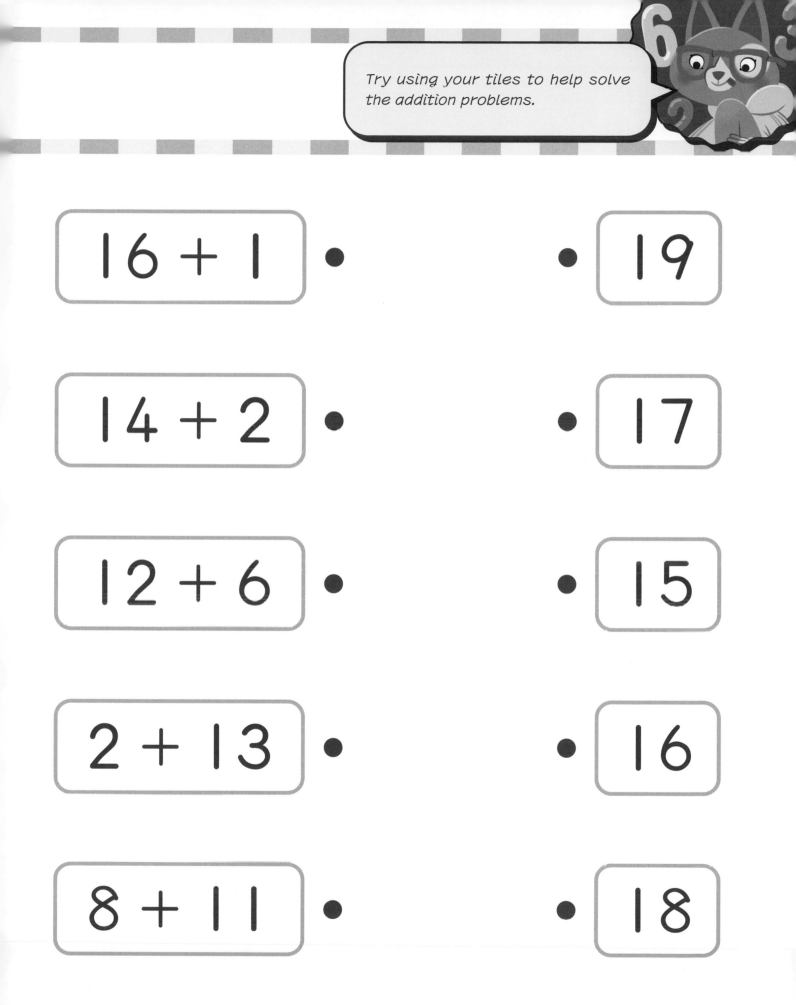

16 + 1 •   • 19

14 + 2 •   • 17

12 + 6 •   • 15

2 + 13 •   • 16

8 + 11 •   • 18

Place a check mark (✔) for correct statements and an "✗" for incorrect statements.

There are a total of 8 islands and dolphins.

There are a total of 14 sailboats and islands.

There is a whale swimming with the dolphins. Can you spot it?

There are a total of 15 sailboats and dolphins.

There are a total of 18 seagulls and sailboats.

How much will each basket of toys cost?
Write the number in the box.

$15

$14

$6

STICKERS STICKERS STICKERS

$3

That will be ☐ dollars.

That will be ☐ dollars.

Which picture completes the scene? Place a check mark (✔) under the correct one.

( )

( )

( )

( )

29

Use your addition skills to play the game!

Start
11+2
☐☐

11+7
☐☐

12+3
☐☐

19+1
☐☐

18+1
☐☐

17+3
☐☐

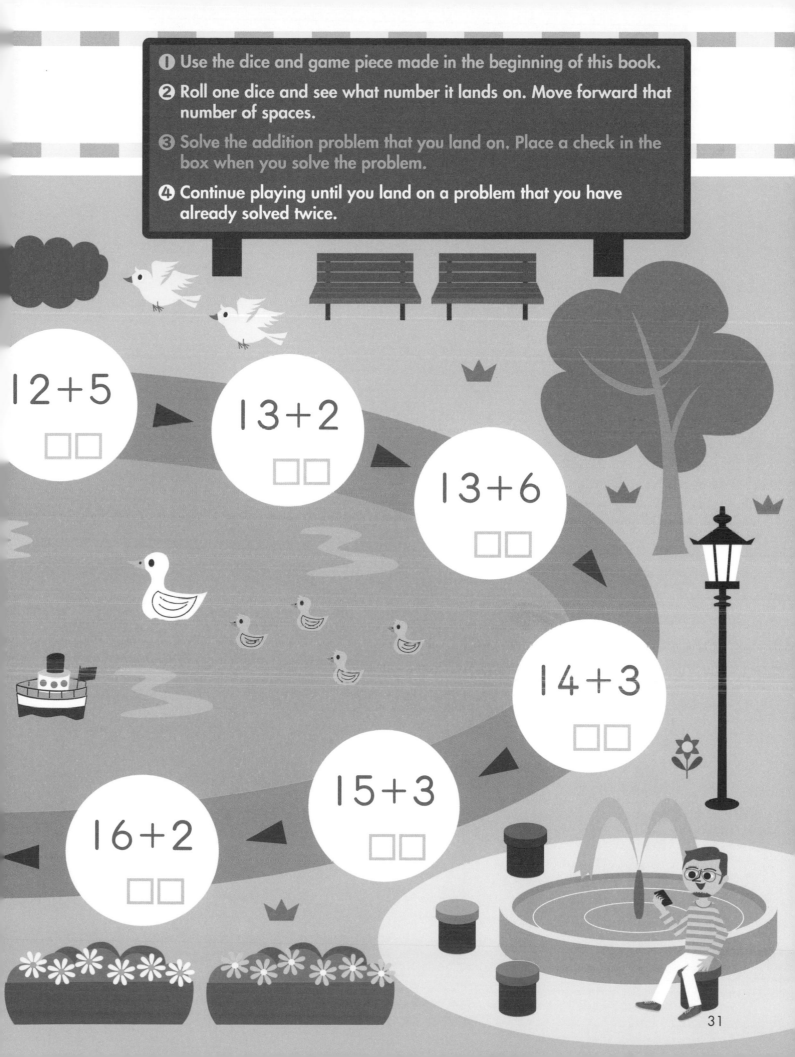

① Use the dice and game piece made in the beginning of this book.

② Roll one dice and see what number it lands on. Move forward that number of spaces.

③ Solve the addition problem that you land on. Place a check in the box when you solve the problem.

④ Continue playing until you land on a problem that you have already solved twice.

12+5 □□

13+2 □□

13+6 □□

14+3 □□

15+3 □□

16+2 □□

Draw a line to the correct answer.

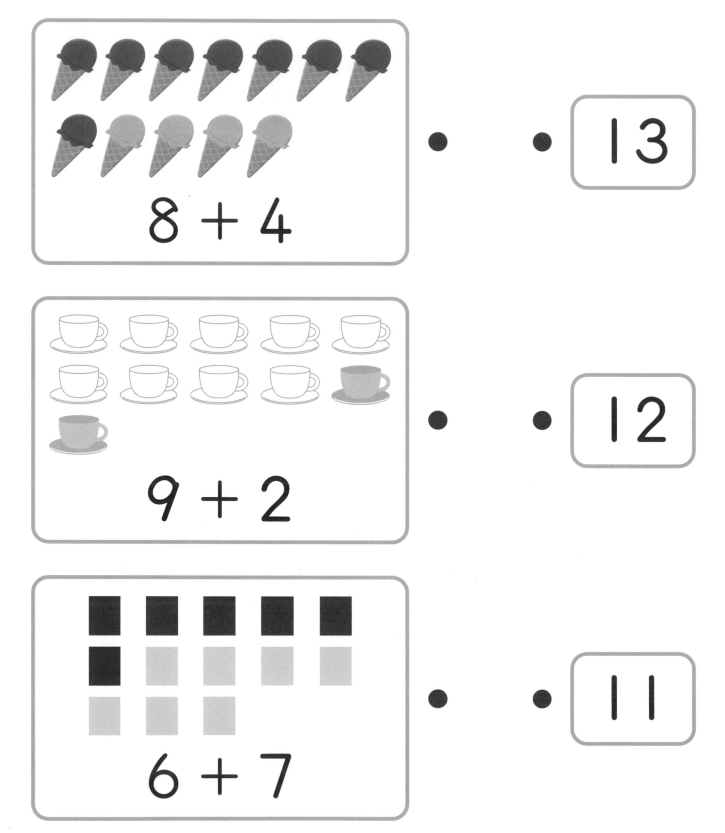

$8 + 4$

$9 + 2$

$6 + 7$

13

12

11

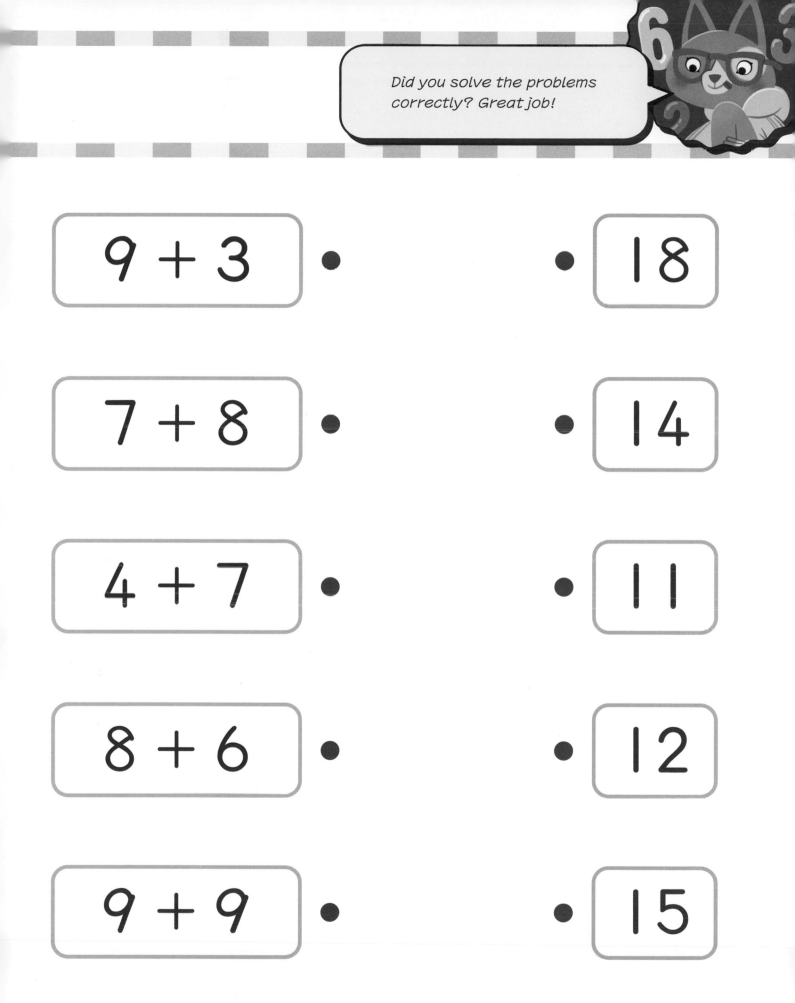

9 + 3 •   • 18

7 + 8 •   • 14

4 + 7 •   • 11

8 + 6 •   • 12

9 + 9 •   • 15

Place a check mark (✓) for correct statements and an "✗" for incorrect statements.

There are a total of 10 snow vehicles and white birds.

There are a total of 13 seals and white birds.

Can you count how many animals there are in total?

There are a total of 14 seals and penguins.

There are a total of 16 white birds and penguins.

17 How much will each basket of school supplies cost? Write the number in the box.

$5

24 COL

GLUE stick   GLUE stick   GLUE stick   GLUE stick   GLUE stick   GLUE stick

$3

$7

Note   No

2 for $3

$4

That will be [ ] dollars.

That will be [ ] dollars.

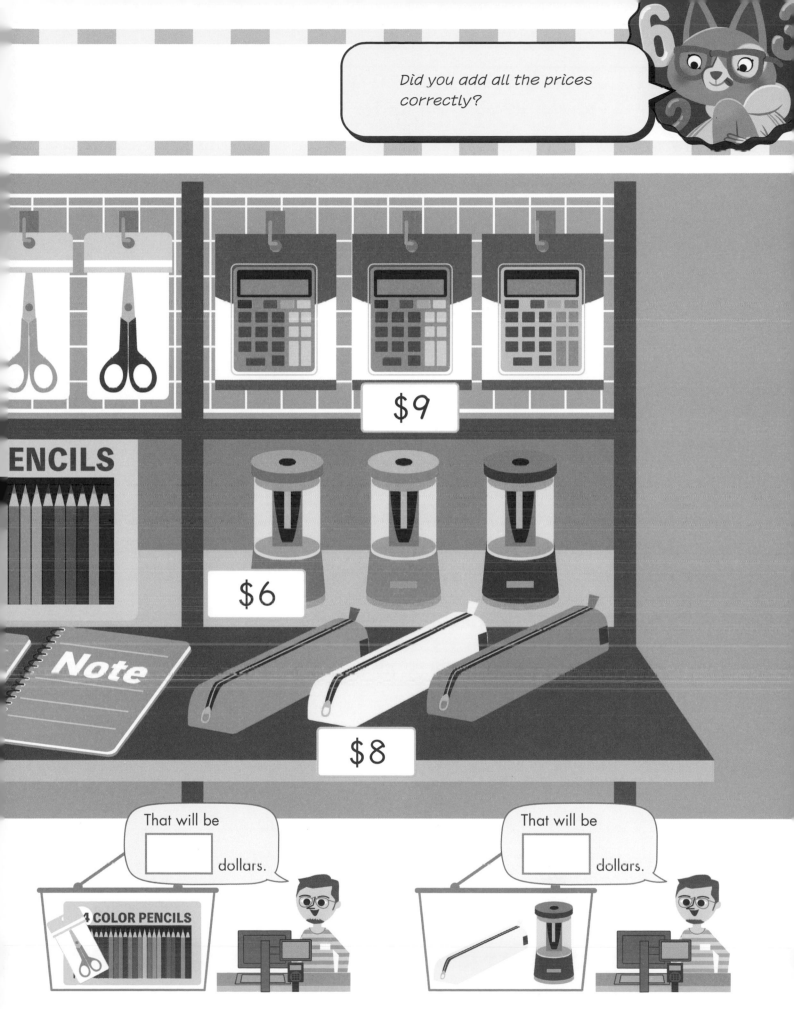

Which picture completes the scene? Place a check mark (✔) under the correct one.

(   )

(   )

It might be helpful to use a piece of scrap paper to add the numbers and solve the comics.

( )

( )

Roll the dice and write the sum of the numbers.

Raya + Noah   Total

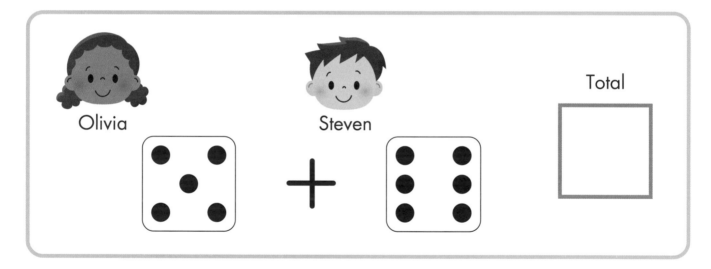

Olivia + Steven   Total

Emma + William   Total

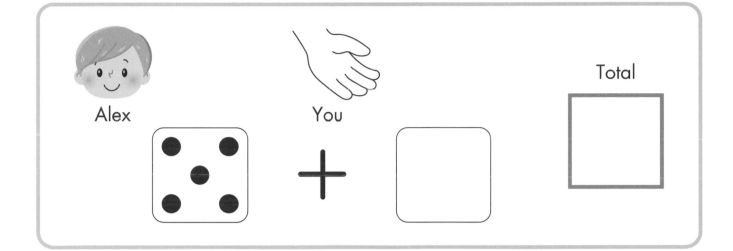

Alex   You   + [ ]   Total [ ]

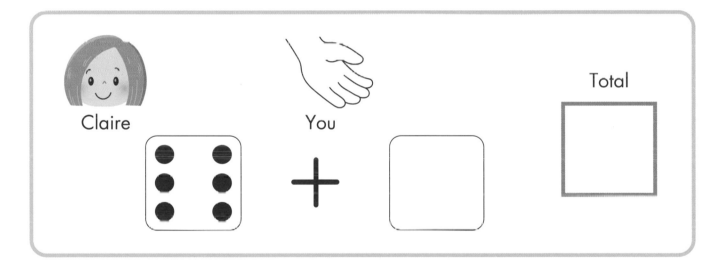

Claire   You   + [ ]   Total [ ]

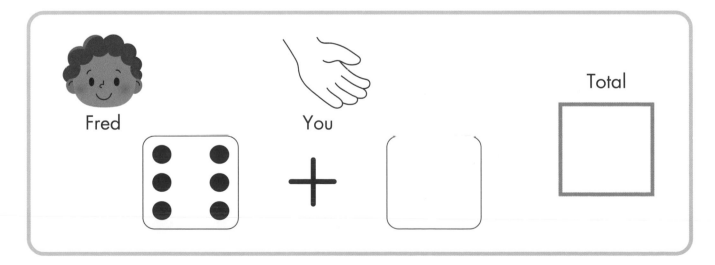

Fred   You   + [ ]   Total [ ]

Draw a line to the correct answer.

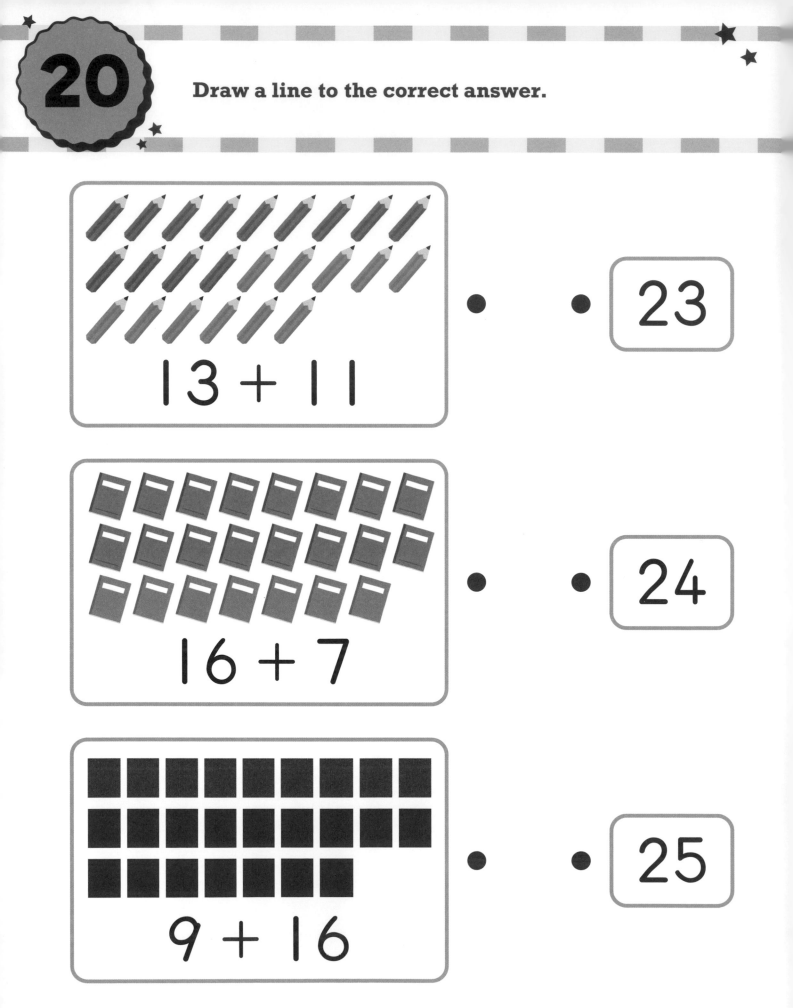

13 + 11

16 + 7

9 + 16

23

24

25

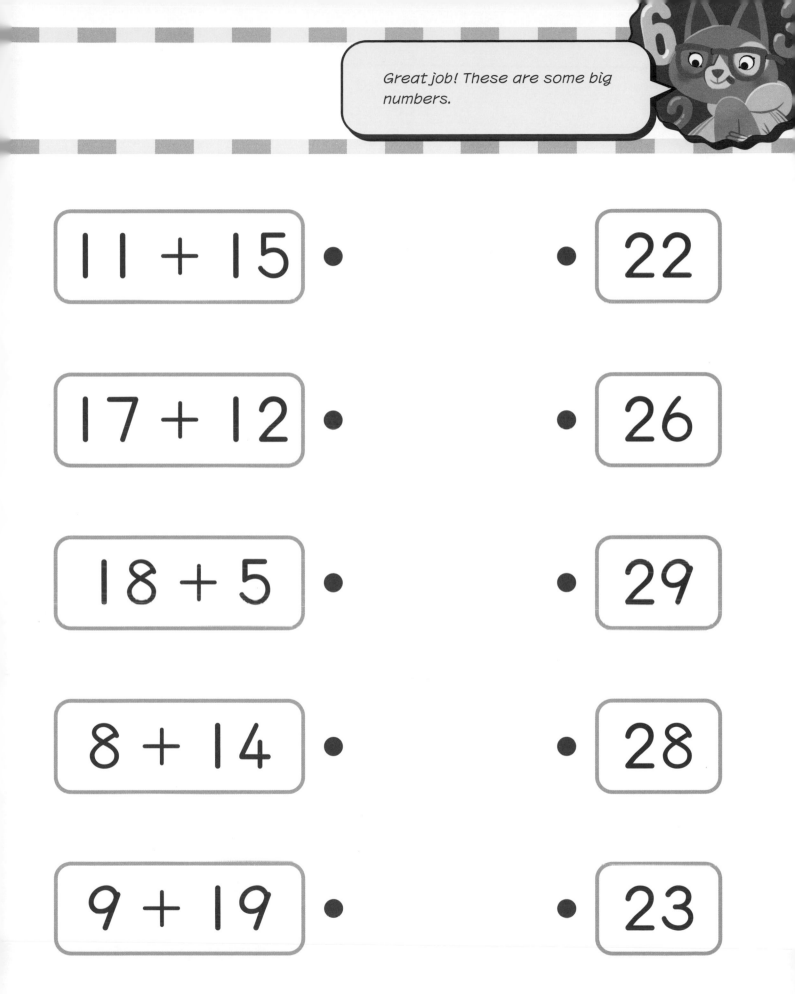

11 + 15 •   • 22

17 + 12 •   • 26

18 + 5 •   • 29

8 + 14 •   • 28

9 + 19 •   • 23

Place a check mark (✓) for correct statements and an "✗" for incorrect statements.

There are a total of 21 BBQ skewers and juice cups.

There are a total of 24 BBQ skewers and birds.

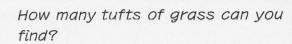

How many tufts of grass can you find?

There are a total of 22 pancakes and juice cups.

There are a total of 25 pancakes and birds.

How much will each basket of books cost? Write the number in the box.

WORLD HISTORY $11

MYSTERY $13

All About Cars $10

EYEWEAR MAGAZINE $12

That will be [ ] dollars.

That will be [ ] dollars.

47

Which picture completes the scene? Place a check mark (✓) under the correct one.

Use your addition skills to play the game!

17+11

18+7

19+5

15+12

16+7

14+14

14+8

❶ Use the dice and game piece made in the beginning of this book.

❷ Roll one dice and see what number it lands on. Move forward that number of spaces.

❸ Solve the addition problem that you land on. Place a check in the box when you solve the problem.

❹ Continue playing until you land on a problem that you have already solved twice.

Start

11+12

11+17

12+9

13+10

12+14

Draw a line to the correct answer.

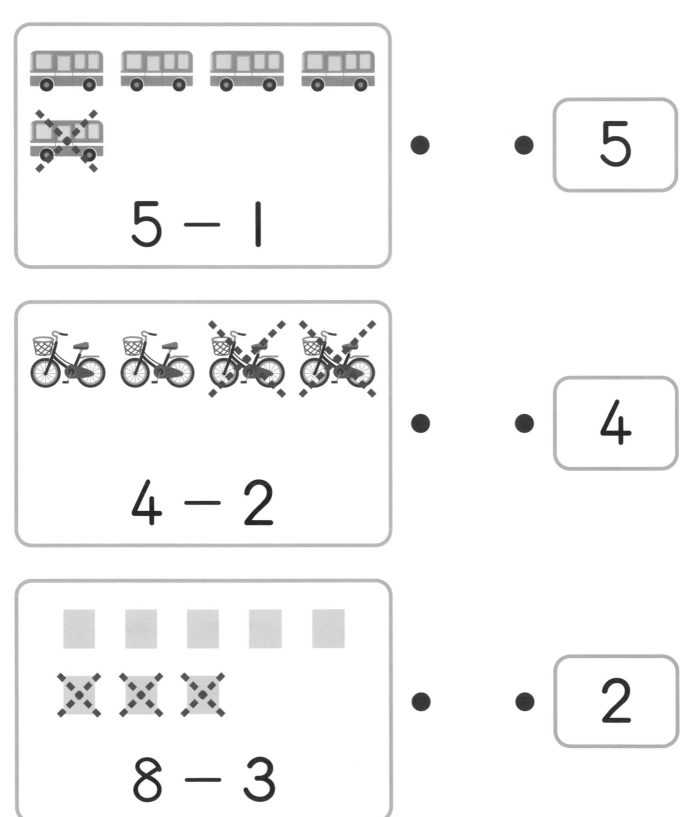

5 − 1

5

4 − 2

4

8 − 3

2

Trace the dotted lines to cross out the number of items you are subtracting. Then see how many remain!

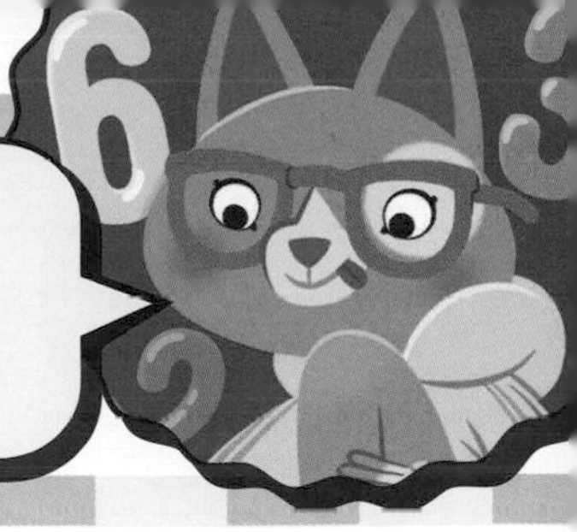

7 − 1	1
5 − 2	3
6 − 4	7
9 − 8	6
10 − 3	2

Draw a line to the correct answer.

You can use a piece of scrap paper to write down the subtraction problem and practice solving.

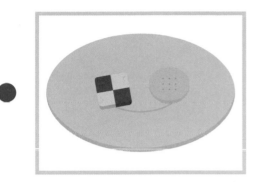

If I eat 5 cookies, how many are left?

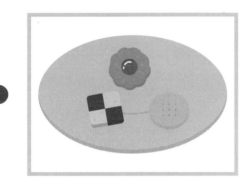

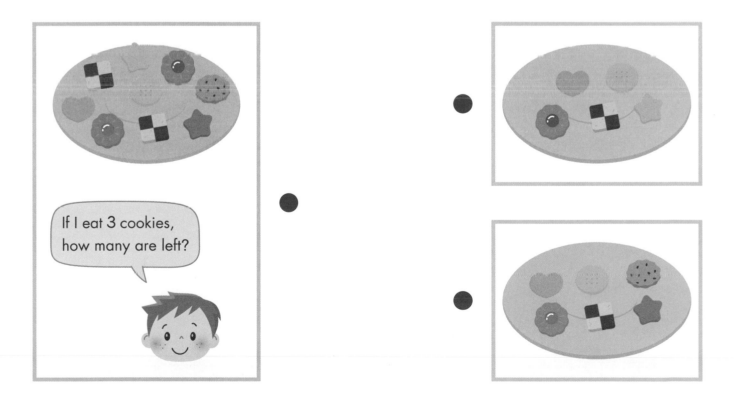

If I eat 3 cookies, how many are left?

Which picture completes the scene? Place a check mark (✔) under the correct one.

(   )

(   )

Do you see pigeons in your local park? Try counting them the next time you see them.

What a beautiful park!

Dad, there are pigeons over there!

There are 5 pigeons.

I wonder if they came to eat.

Oh, 4 pigeons flew away!

How many pigeons are left?

?

Let's see, there is 1 pigeon left!

Maybe they will all come back here again.

( )

Let's see, there are 9 pigeons!

Maybe they will all come back here again.

( )

57

28

Draw a line to the correct answer.

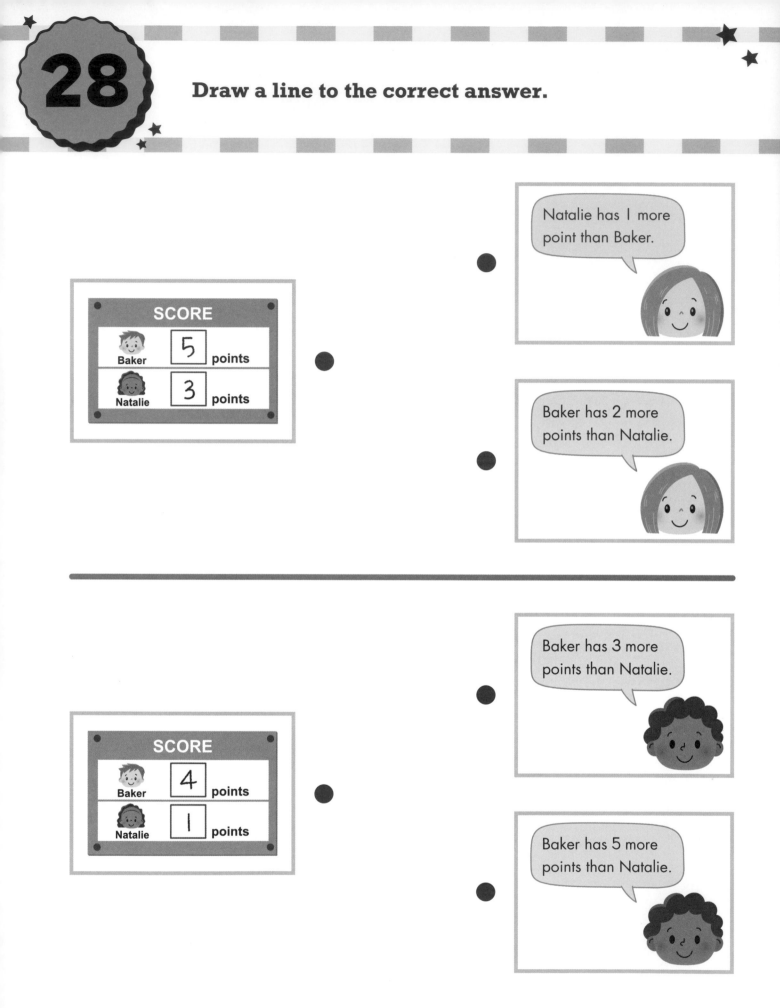

Remember, you can always use your tiles to help you count.

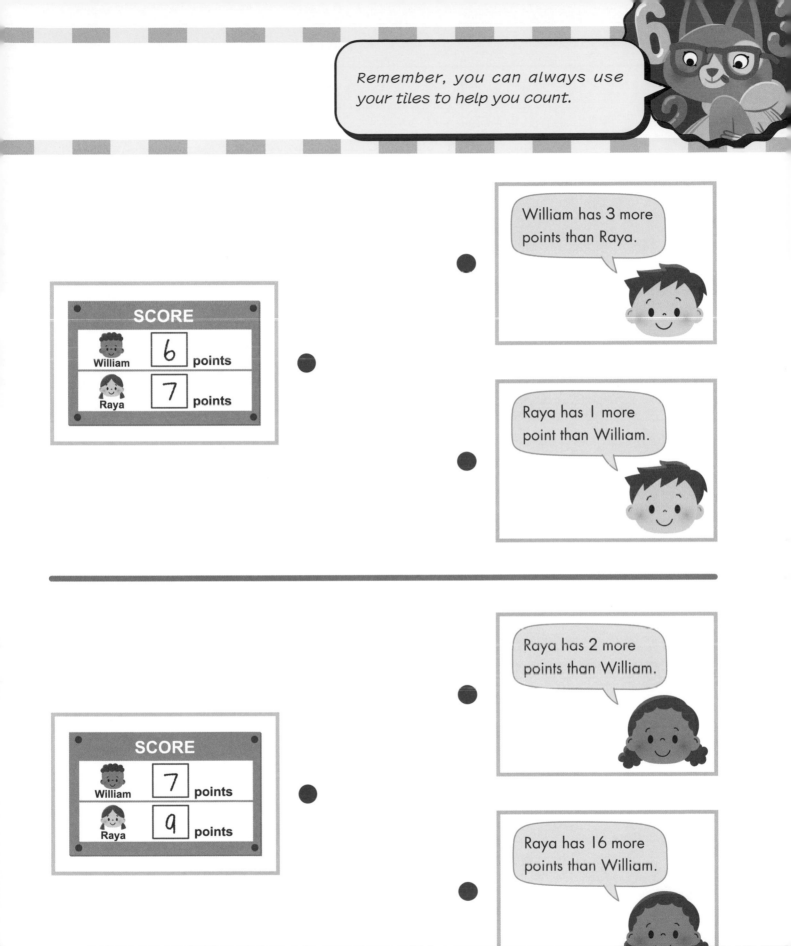

William has 3 more points than Raya.

Raya has 1 more point than William.

SCORE

William 6 points

Raya 7 points

Raya has 2 more points than William.

Raya has 16 more points than William.

SCORE

William 7 points

Raya 9 points

Place a check mark (✓) for correct statements and an "✗" for incorrect statements.

There are 2 more candles than hats.

There are 6 more whipped cream swirls than hats.

What is your favorite type of cake?

There are 4 more whipped cream swirls than candles.

There are 5 more strawberries than candles.

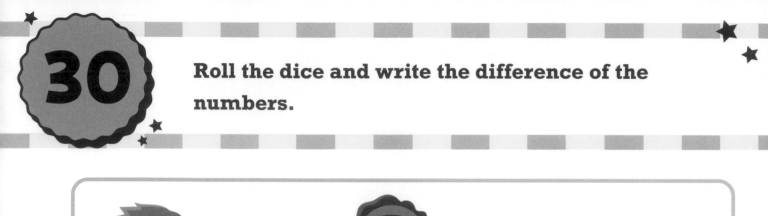

30

Roll the dice and write the difference of the numbers.

Baker   Natalie   Difference

[5] — [1] = 4

Noah   Emma   Difference

[4] — [2] = [ ]

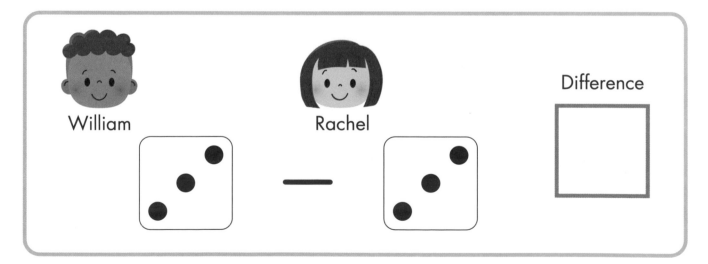

William   Rachel   Difference

[4] — [3] = [ ]

Use the dice you made from page 1. If the dice rolled by the two players comes out the same, the difference is 0 (zero).

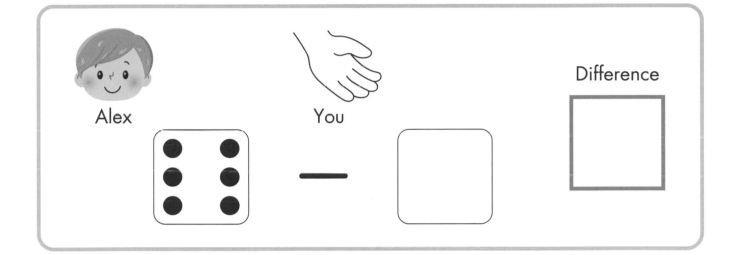

Alex   You   Difference

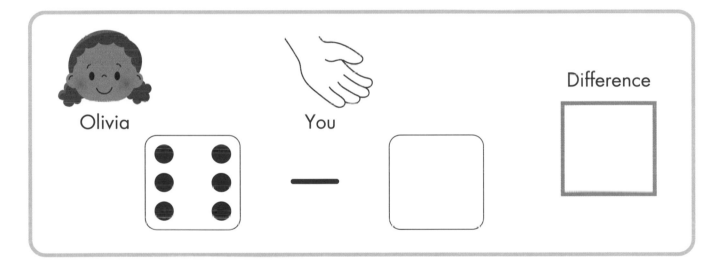

Olivia   You   Difference

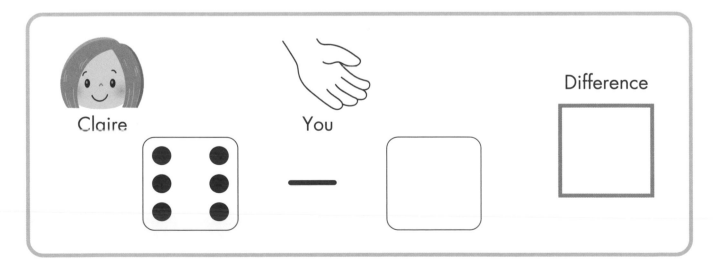

Claire   You   Difference

31

Draw a line to the correct answer.

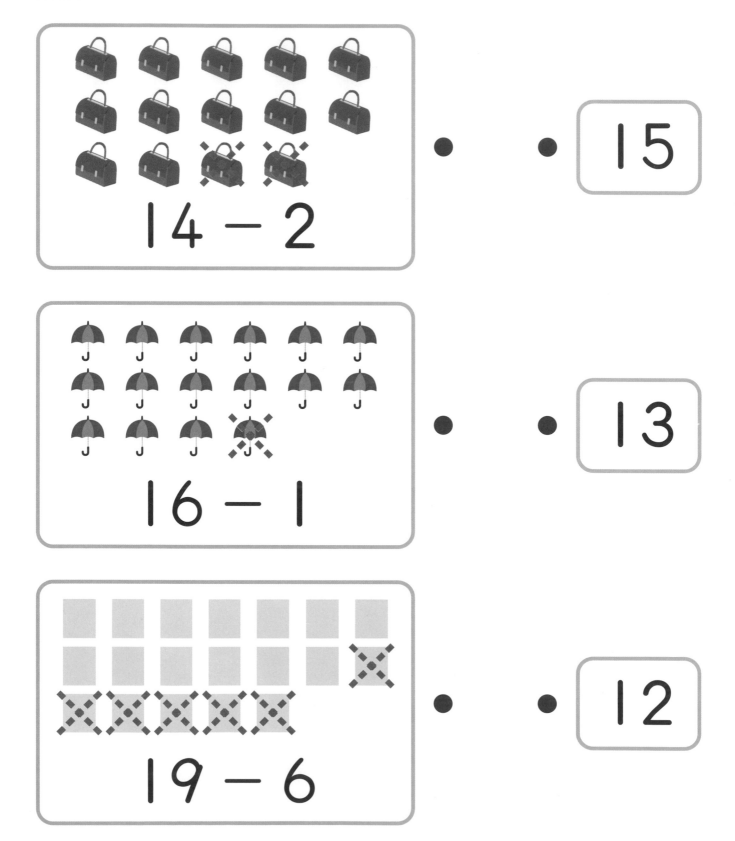

14 − 2

15

16 − 1

13

19 − 6

12

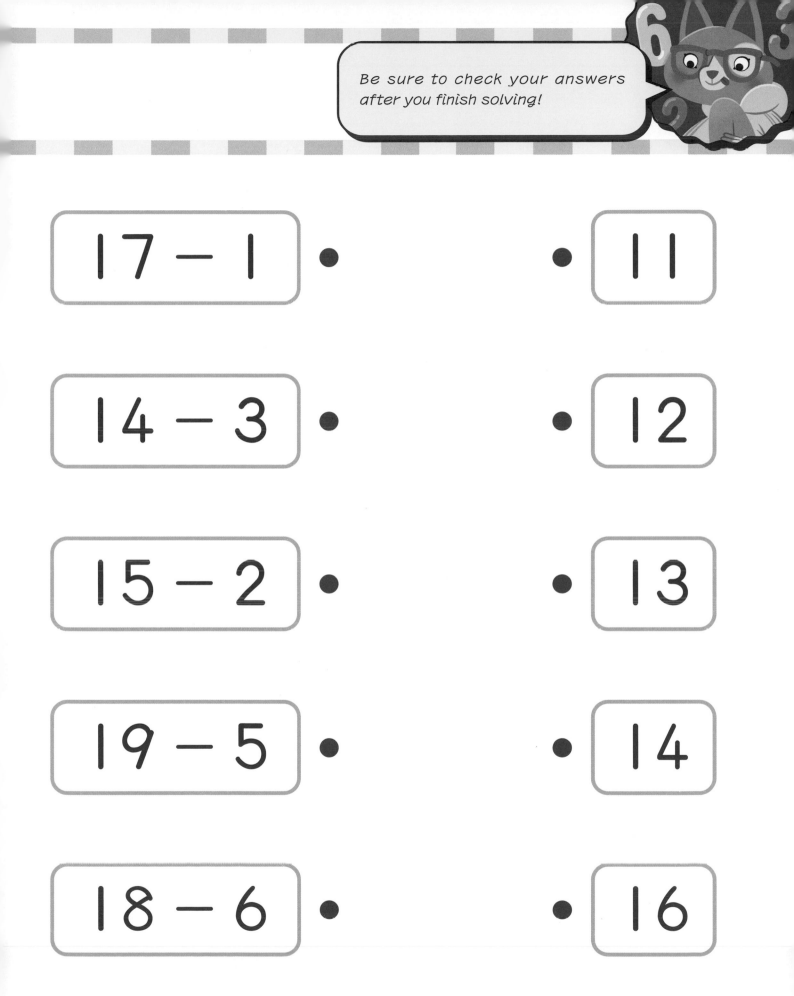

Draw a line to the correct answer.

Try crossing out or drawing an "x" over the objects being eaten or returned.

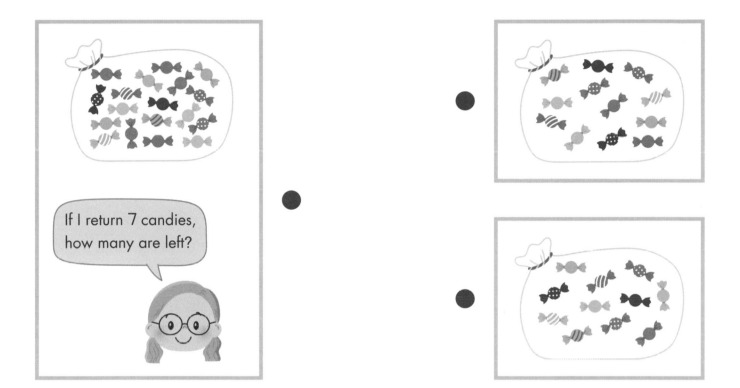

If I return 7 candies, how many are left?

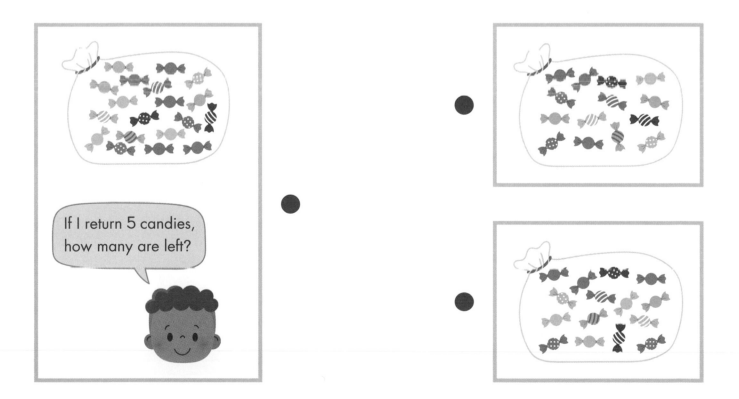

If I return 5 candies, how many are left?

Which picture completes the scene? Place a check mark (✓) under the correct one.

I can't wait to get to the stadium!

I'm so excited for today's baseball game.

I wonder where everyone is going.

There are 14 passengers on this bus right now, including us.

Oh, we stopped at a bus stop.

Look, 2 passengers are getting off here.

?

That means the number of people on the bus right now is...

12 people.

(   )

That means the number of people on the bus right now is...

16 people.

(   )

( )

( )

Draw a line to the correct answer.

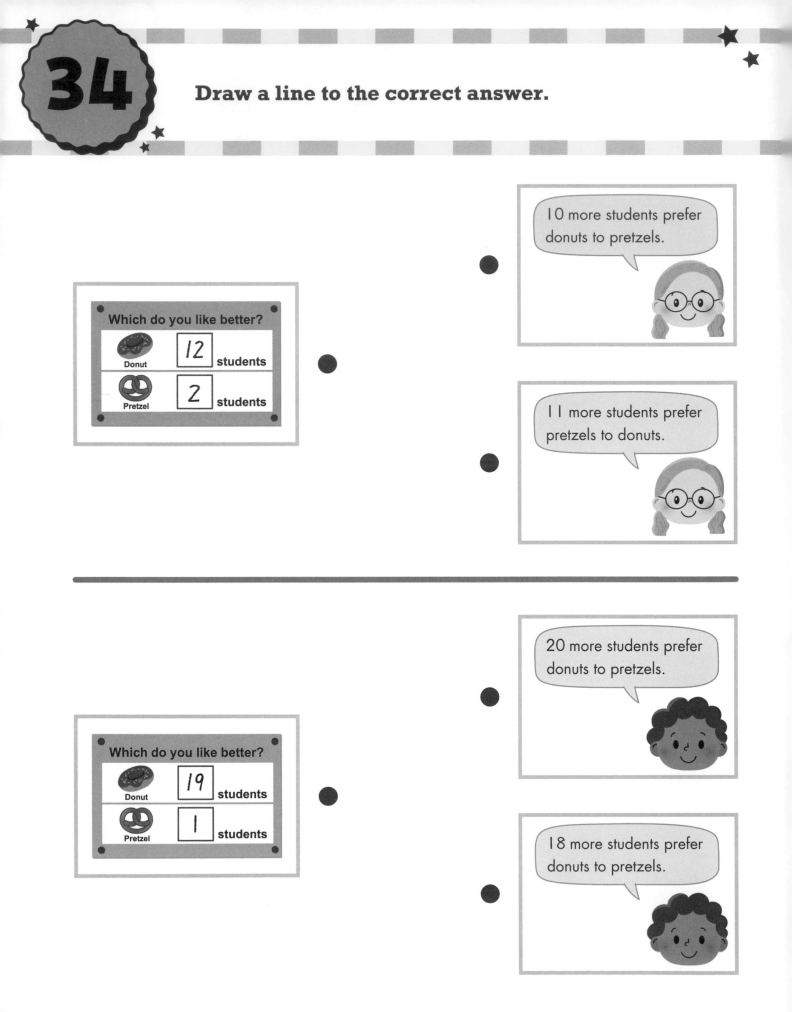

10 more students prefer donuts to pretzels.

Which do you like better?
Donut 12 students
Pretzel 2 students

11 more students prefer pretzels to donuts.

20 more students prefer donuts to pretzels.

Which do you like better?
Donut 19 students
Pretzel 1 students

18 more students prefer donuts to pretzels.

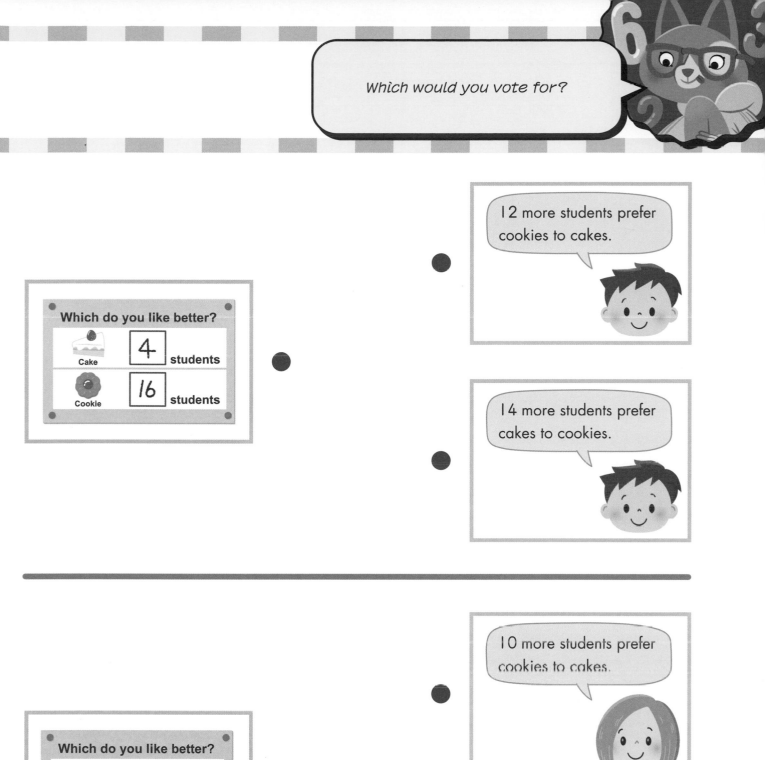

Which do you like better?

Cake	4	students
Cookie	16	students

12 more students prefer cookies to cakes.

14 more students prefer cakes to cookies.

Which do you like better?

Cake	6	students
Cookie	17	students

10 more students prefer cookies to cakes.

11 more students prefer cookies to cakes.

35

Place a check mark (✔) for correct statements and an "✗" for incorrect statements.

There are 13 more cars than trees.

There are 13 more cars than street lights.

72

Buildings and cars come in all colors and shapes!

There are 10 more buildings than trees.

There are 10 more buildings than street lights.

73

Use your subtraction skills to play the game!

13 − 1

14 − 2

12 − 1

Start

11 − 1

19 − 3

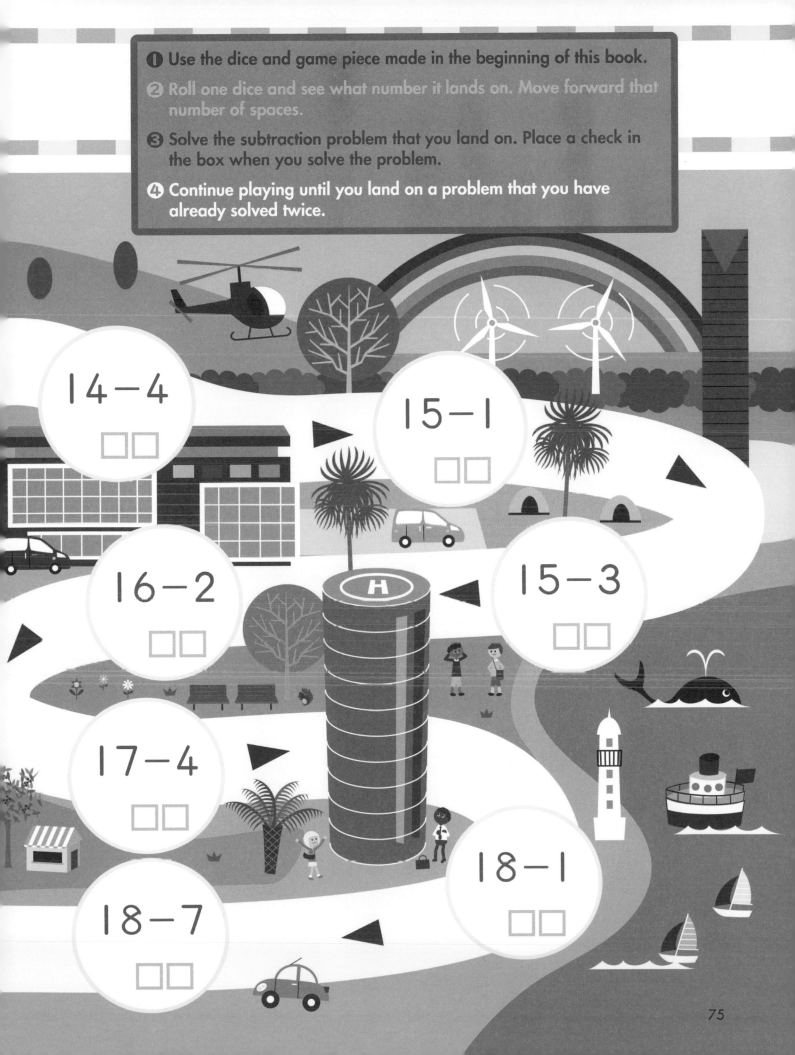

❶ Use the dice and game piece made in the beginning of this book.

❷ Roll one dice and see what number it lands on. Move forward that number of spaces.

❸ Solve the subtraction problem that you land on. Place a check in the box when you solve the problem.

❹ Continue playing until you land on a problem that you have already solved twice.

14 − 4

15 − 1

16 − 2

15 − 3

17 − 4

18 − 1

18 − 7

Draw a line to the correct answer.

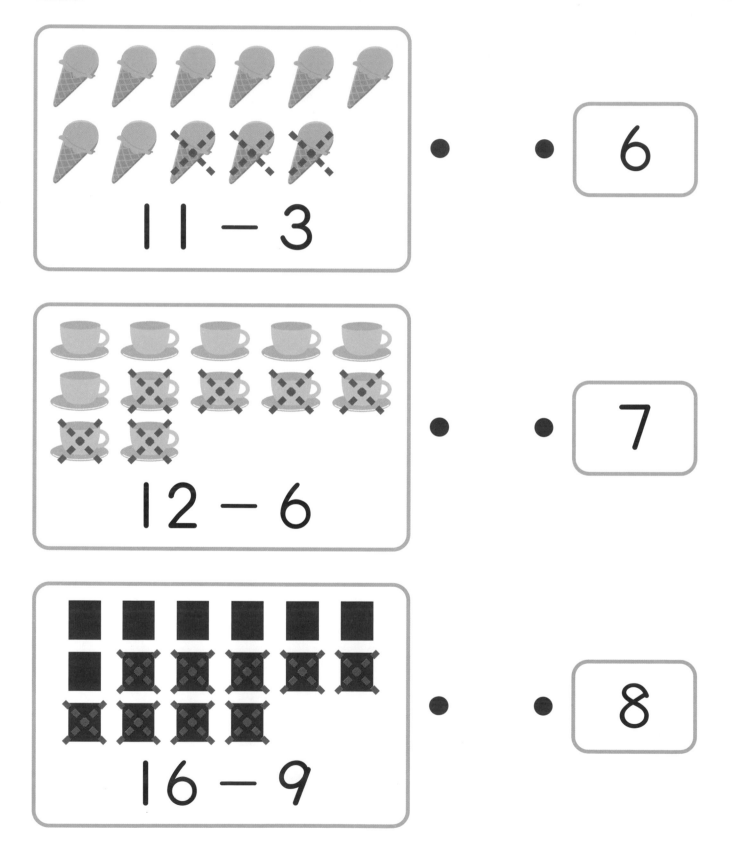

11 − 3

6

12 − 6

7

16 − 9

8

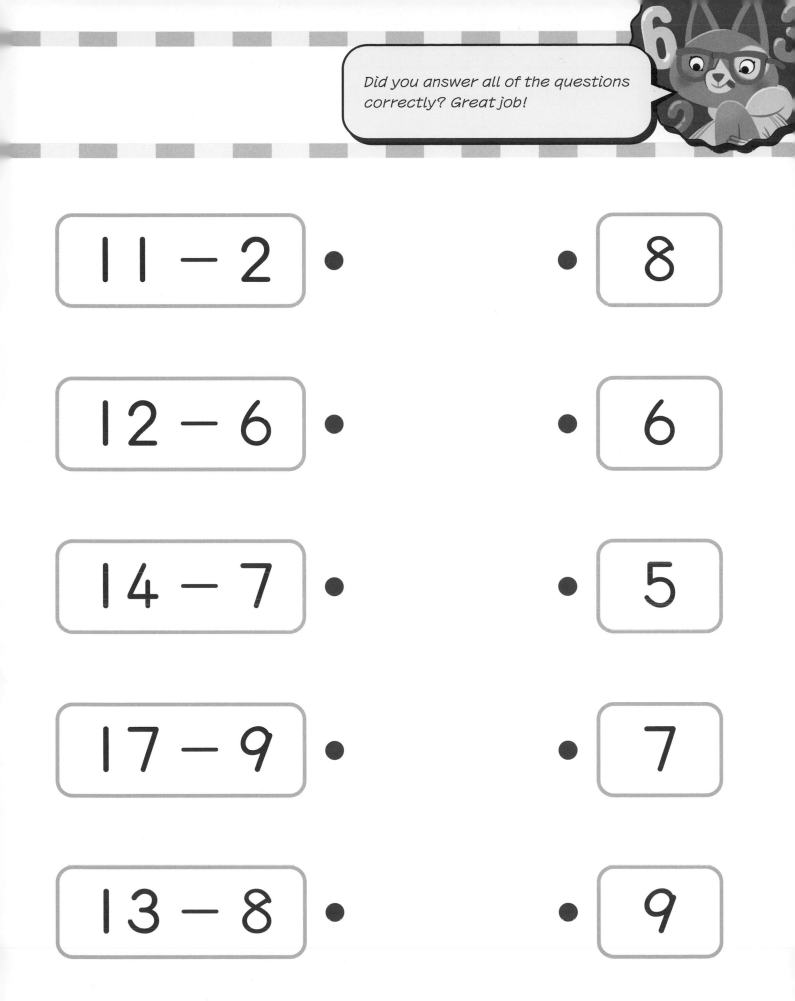

11 − 2 ● ● 8

12 − 6 ● ● 6

14 − 7 ● ● 5

17 − 9 ● ● 7

13 − 8 ● ● 9

Draw a line to the correct answer.

If I eat 2 sausages, how many are left?

If I eat 5 sausages, how many are left?

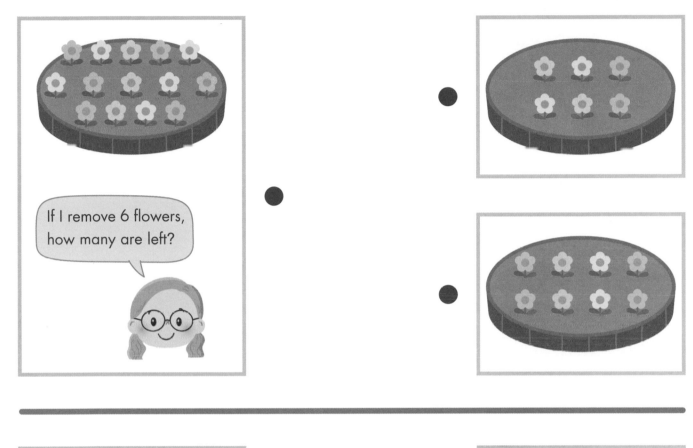

If I remove 6 flowers, how many are left?

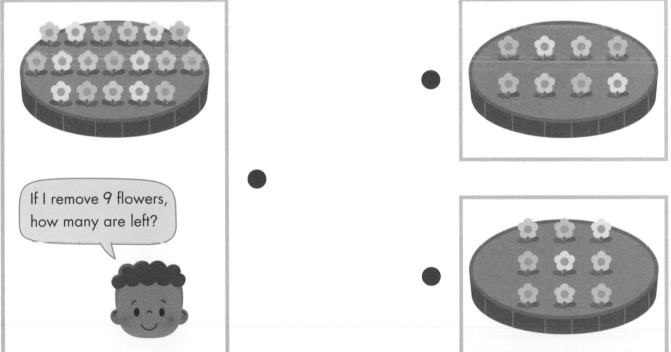

If I remove 9 flowers, how many are left?

Which picture completes the scene? Place a check mark (✓) under the correct one.

We have plenty of eggs, so let's make sunny-side up again today.

I think we have 12 eggs left.

Sophia, can you bring me 3 eggs from the fridge?

Of course.

Ah!

My hand slipped. I cracked all 3 eggs. So sorry, Mom.

?

We can use the broken eggs, too.

After using these eggs, there are 8 eggs left.

( )

We can use the broken eggs, too.

After using these eggs, there are 9 eggs left.

( )

( )

( )

40 **Draw a line to the correct answer.**

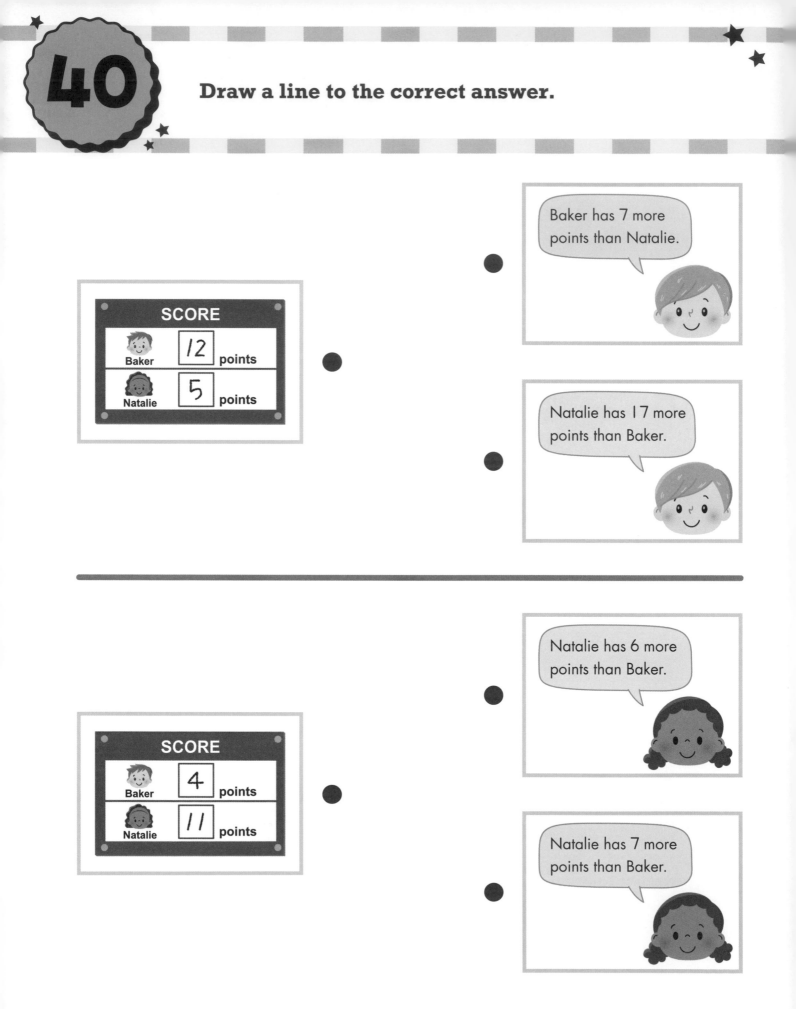

SCORE

Baker 12 points

Natalie 5 points

Baker has 7 more points than Natalie.

Natalie has 17 more points than Baker.

SCORE

Baker 4 points

Natalie 11 points

Natalie has 6 more points than Baker.

Natalie has 7 more points than Baker.

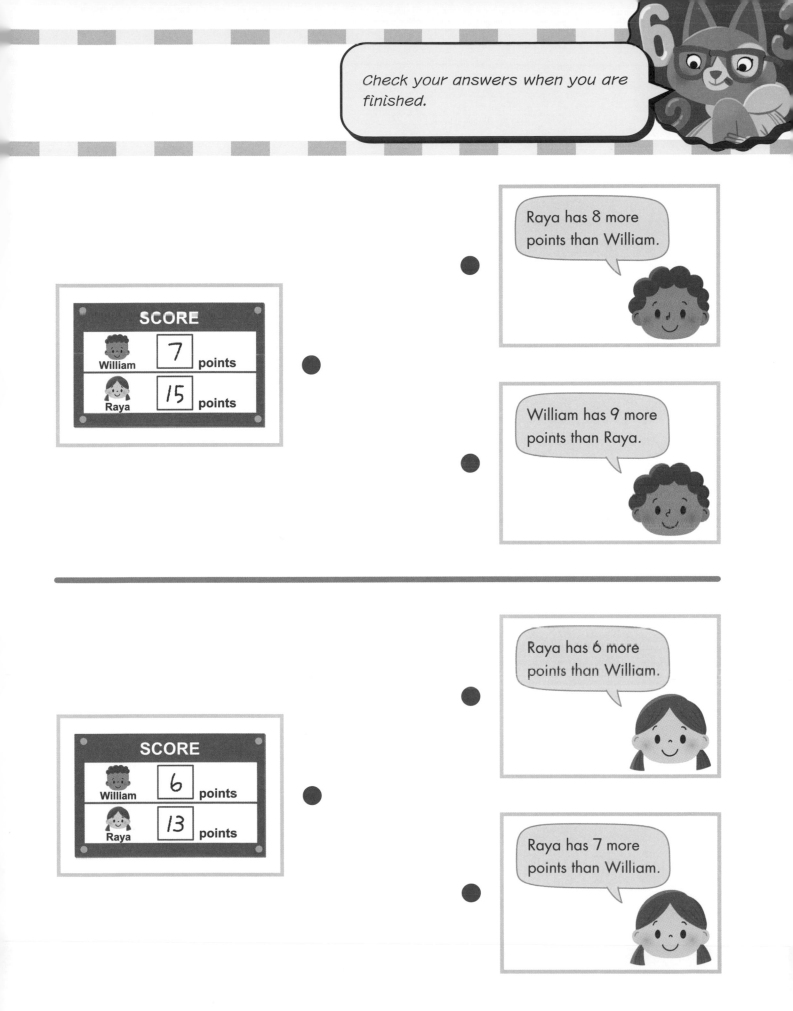

SCORE

William 7 points
Raya 15 points

Raya has 8 more points than William.

William has 9 more points than Raya.

SCORE

William 6 points
Raya 13 points

Raya has 6 more points than William.

Raya has 7 more points than William.

41 Place a check mark (✓) for correct statements and an "✗" for incorrect statements.

BLUE CANDY

There are 4 more jelly beans than blue candies.

☐

There are 7 more jelly beans than lollipops.

☐

Did you count all of the candy correctly? Which candy is your favorite?

JELLY BEAN

GUMBALL

There are 3 more gumballs than blue candies.

There are 5 more gumballs than lollipops.

42

Roll the dice and write the difference of the numbers.

Noah — Natalie

Difference

7

Alex — Claire

Difference

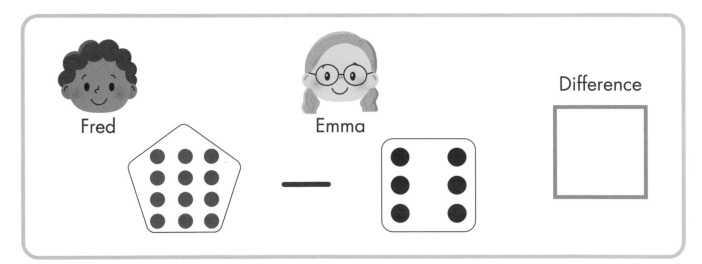

Fred — Emma

Difference

There are different types of dice. Here they are using a 12-sided dice. Look carefully at the number of dots on the dice.

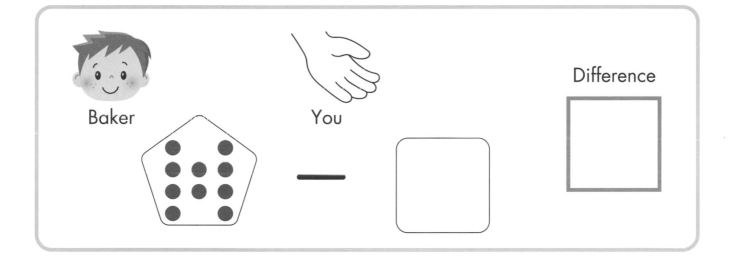

Baker

You

Difference

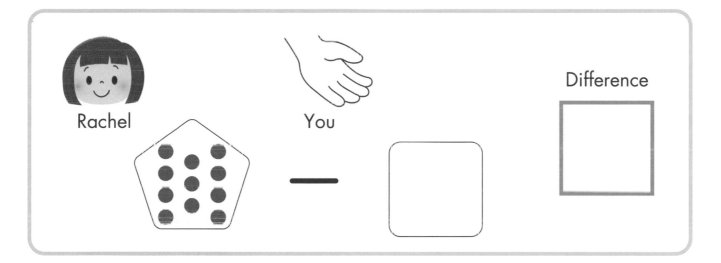

Rachel

You

Difference

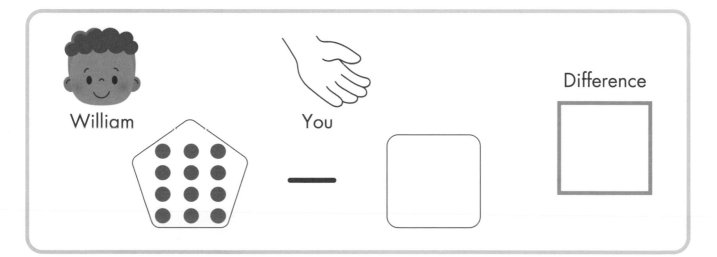

William

You

Difference

43

Draw a line to the correct answer.

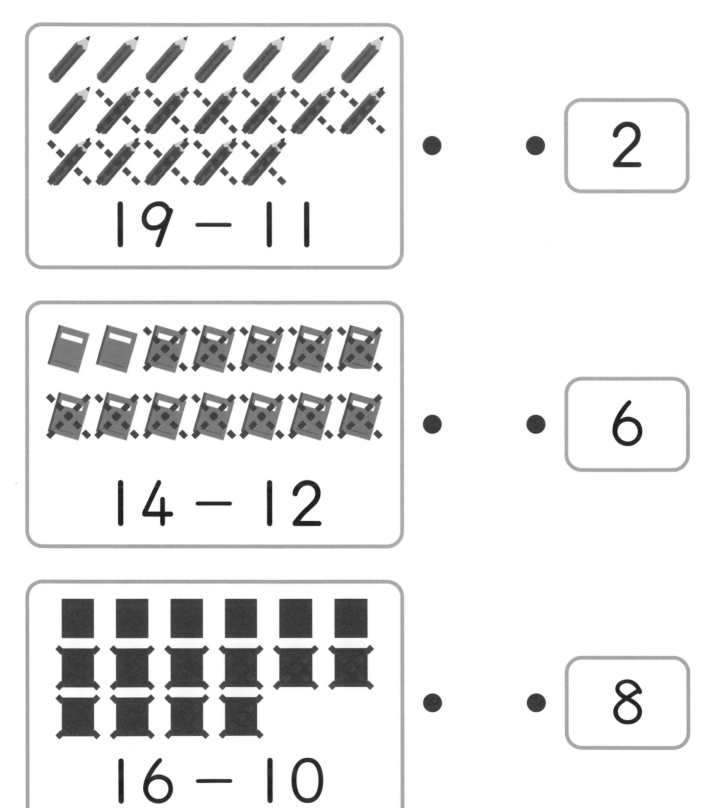

19 − 11

2

14 − 12

6

16 − 10

8

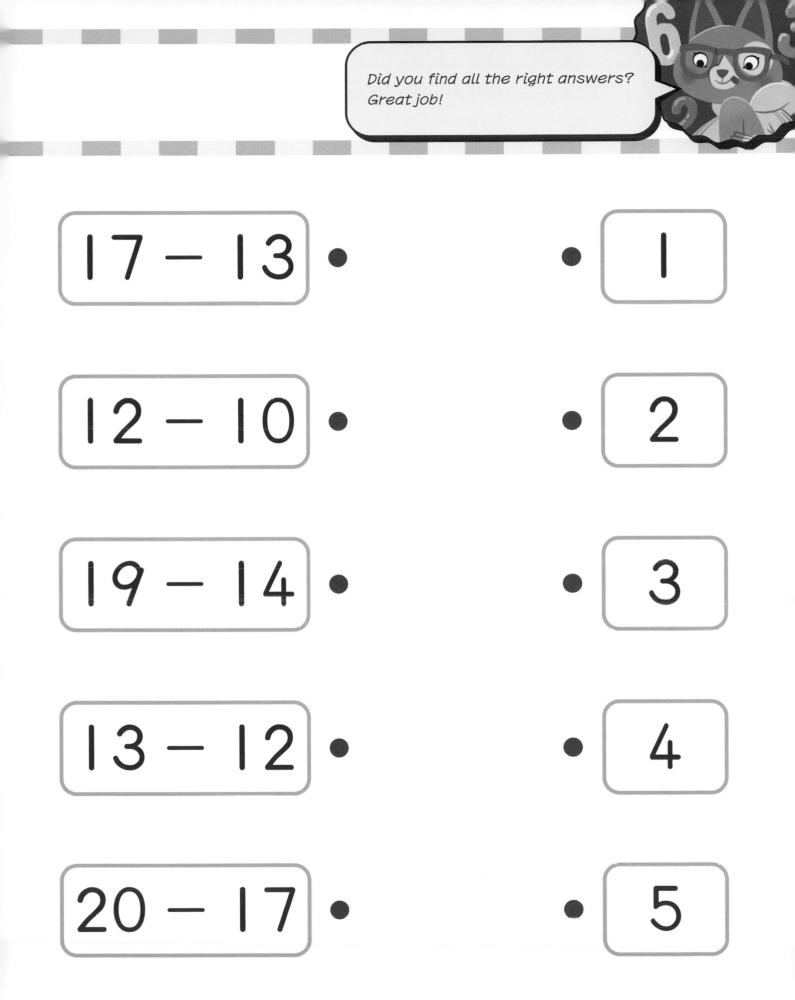

17 − 13 •   • 1

12 − 10 •   • 2

19 − 14 •   • 3

13 − 12 •   • 4

20 − 17 •   • 5

**Draw a line to the correct answer.**

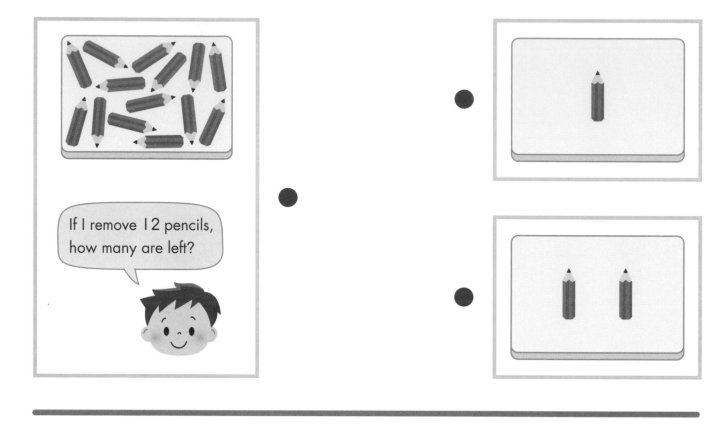

If I remove 12 pencils, how many are left?

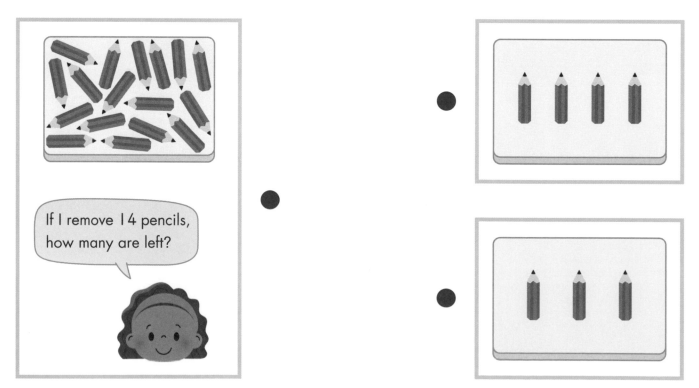

If I remove 14 pencils, how many are left?

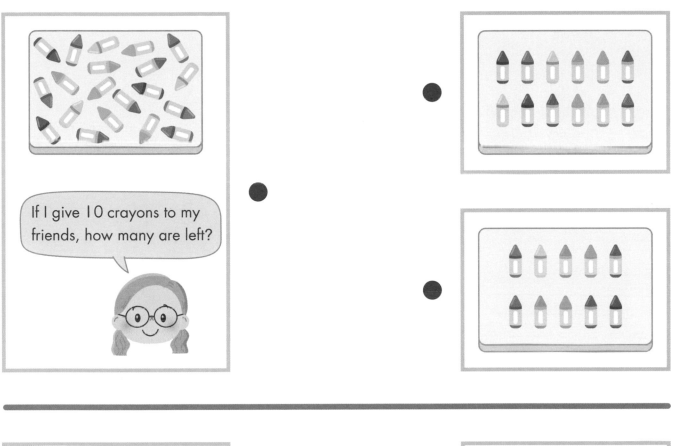

Remember, you can use the tiles to help you count.

If I give 10 crayons to my friends, how many are left?

If I give 11 crayons to my friends, how many are left?

Which picture completes the scene? Place a check mark (✔) under the correct one.

( )

( )

( )

( )

Draw a line to the correct answer.

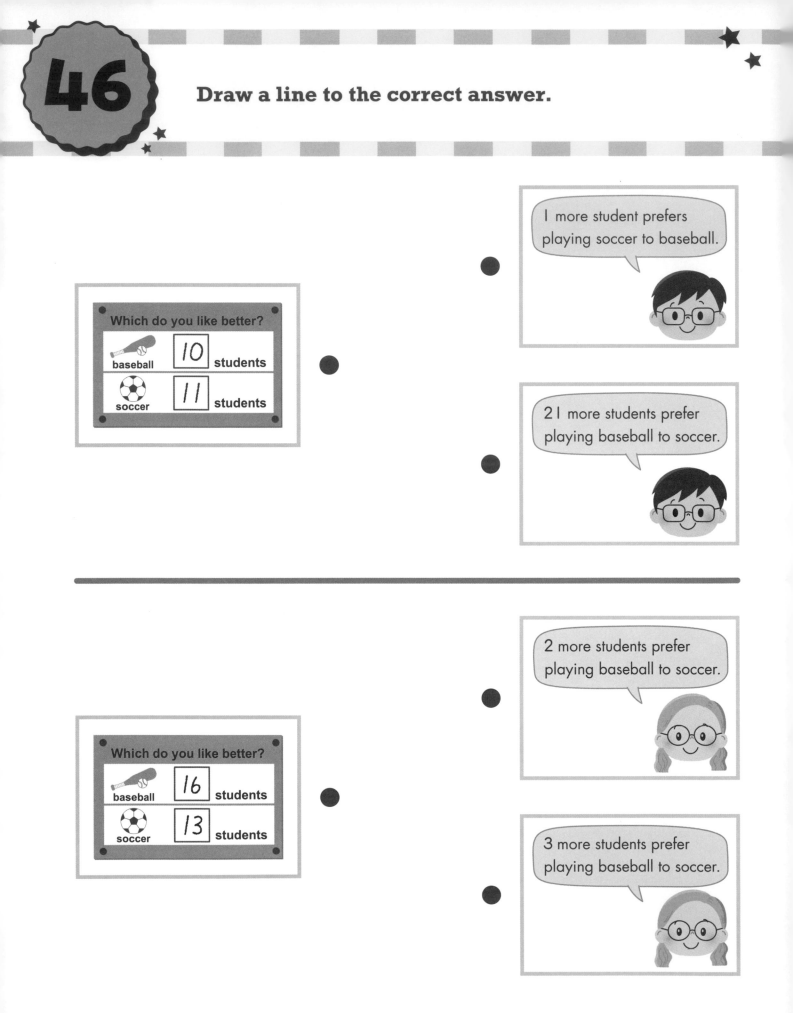

Which do you like better?

baseball 10 students

soccer 11 students

1 more student prefers playing soccer to baseball.

21 more students prefer playing baseball to soccer.

Which do you like better?

baseball 16 students

soccer 13 students

2 more students prefer playing baseball to soccer.

3 more students prefer playing baseball to soccer.

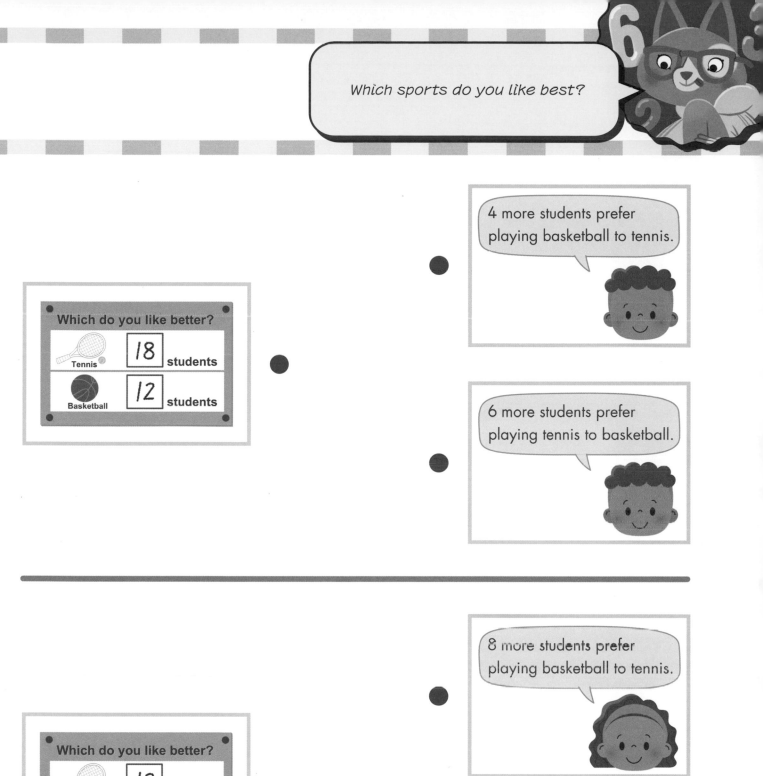

Which do you like better?

Tennis	18	students
Basketball	12	students

4 more students prefer playing basketball to tennis.

6 more students prefer playing tennis to basketball.

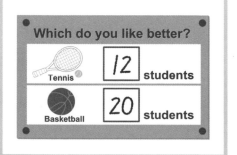

Which do you like better?

Tennis	12	students
Basketball	20	students

8 more students prefer playing basketball to tennis.

18 more students prefer playing basketball to tennis.

Place a check mark (✓) for correct statements and an "✗" for incorrect statements.

There is 1 more white tulip than there are pink tulips.

There are 2 more yellow tulips than pink tulips.

There are 3 more yellow tulips than white tulips.

There are 7 more red tulips than white tulips.

48

Use your subtraction skills to play the game!

14 − 11 □□

14 − 13 □□

13 − 12 □□

15 − 12 □□

12 − 10 □□

Start 11 − 10 □□

Zoo

1. Use the dice and game piece made in the beginning of this book.
2. Roll one dice and see what number it lands on. Move forward that number of spaces.
3. Solve the subtraction problem that you land on. Place a check in the box when you solve the problem.
4. Continue playing until you land on a problem that you have already solved twice.

17−12 □□

16−14 □□

18−14 □□

16−10 □□

19−11 □□

19−18 □□

Draw a line to the correct answer.

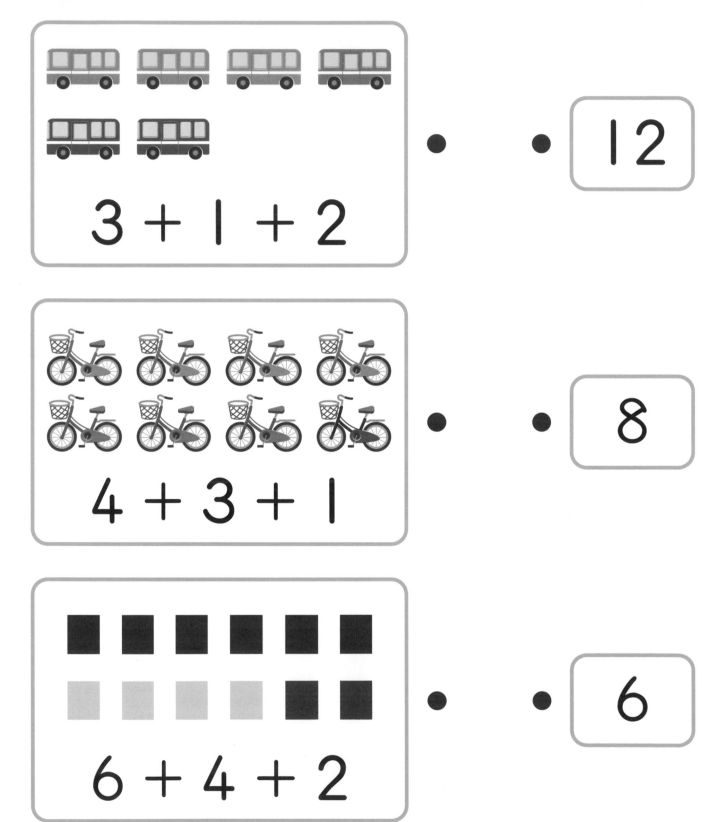

$3 + 1 + 2$

12

$4 + 3 + 1$

8

$6 + 4 + 2$

6

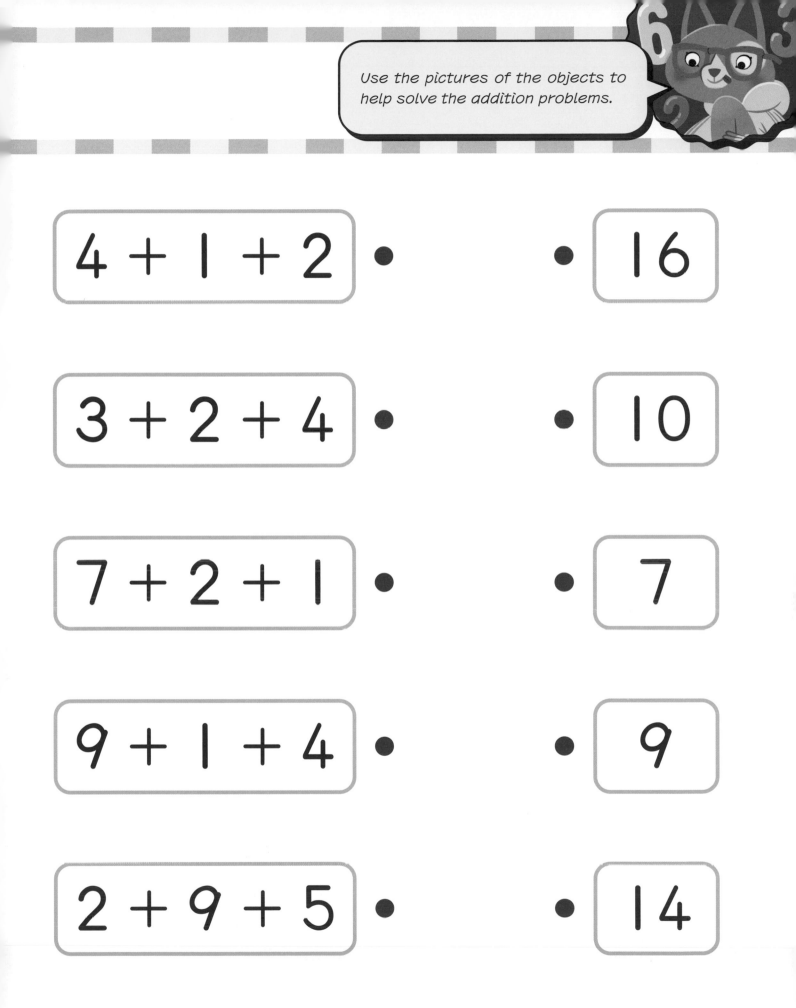

4 + 1 + 2 •   • 16

3 + 2 + 4 •   • 10

7 + 2 + 1 •   • 7

9 + 1 + 4 •   • 9

2 + 9 + 5 •   • 14

Place a check mark (✓) for correct statements and an "✗" for incorrect statements.

There are a total of 12 airplanes, houses, and balloons.

There are a total of 16 airplanes, balloons, and birds.

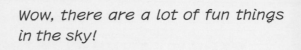

Wow, there are a lot of fun things in the sky!

There are a total of 18 houses, balloons, and birds.

There are a total of 20 houses, hot-air ballons, and birds.

How much will each basket of snacks cost?
Write the number in the box.

Draw a line to the correct answer.

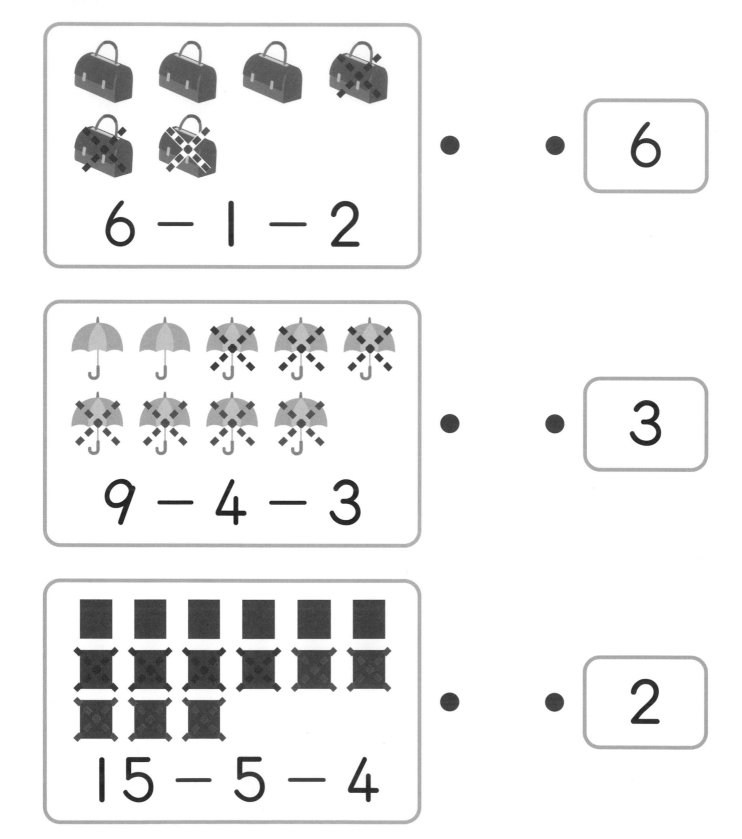

6 – 1 – 2

6

9 – 4 – 3

3

15 – 5 – 4

2

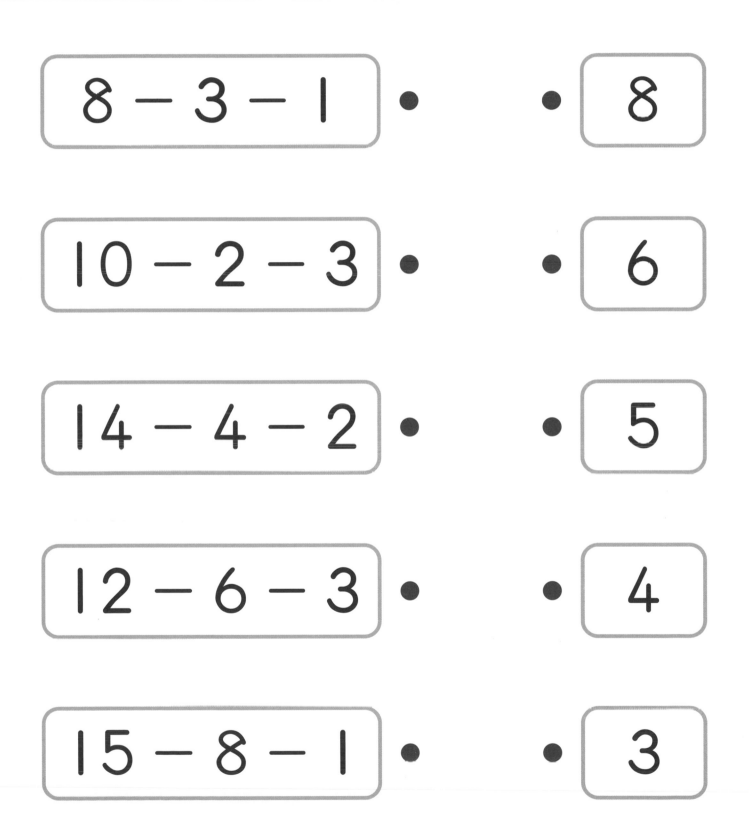

8 – 3 – 1 • • 8

10 – 2 – 3 • • 6

14 – 4 – 2 • • 5

12 – 6 – 3 • • 4

15 – 8 – 1 • • 3

53

Draw a line to the correct answer.

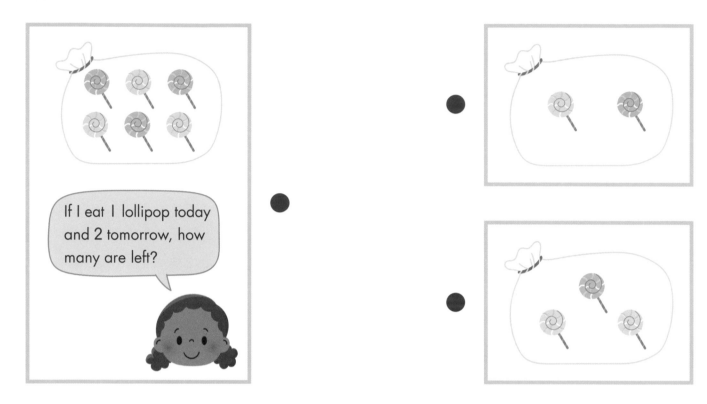

If I eat 1 lollipop today and 2 tomorrow, how many are left?

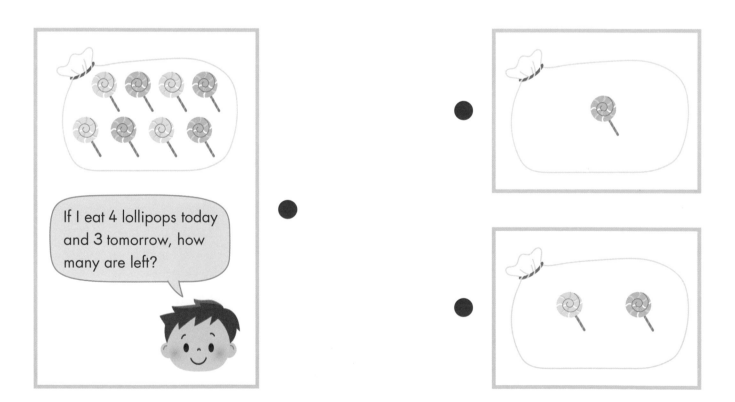

If I eat 4 lollipops today and 3 tomorrow, how many are left?

If I give 1 tulip to a friend today and 3 tomorrow, how many are left?

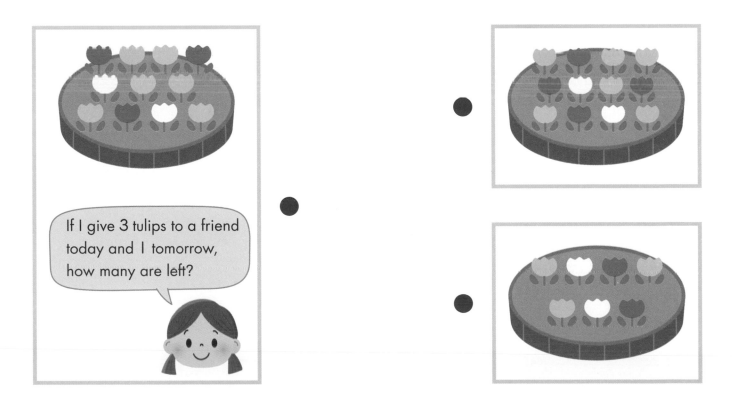

If I give 3 tulips to a friend today and 1 tomorrow, how many are left?

Which picture completes the scene? Place a check mark (✓) under the correct one.

( )

( )

Draw a line to the correct answer.

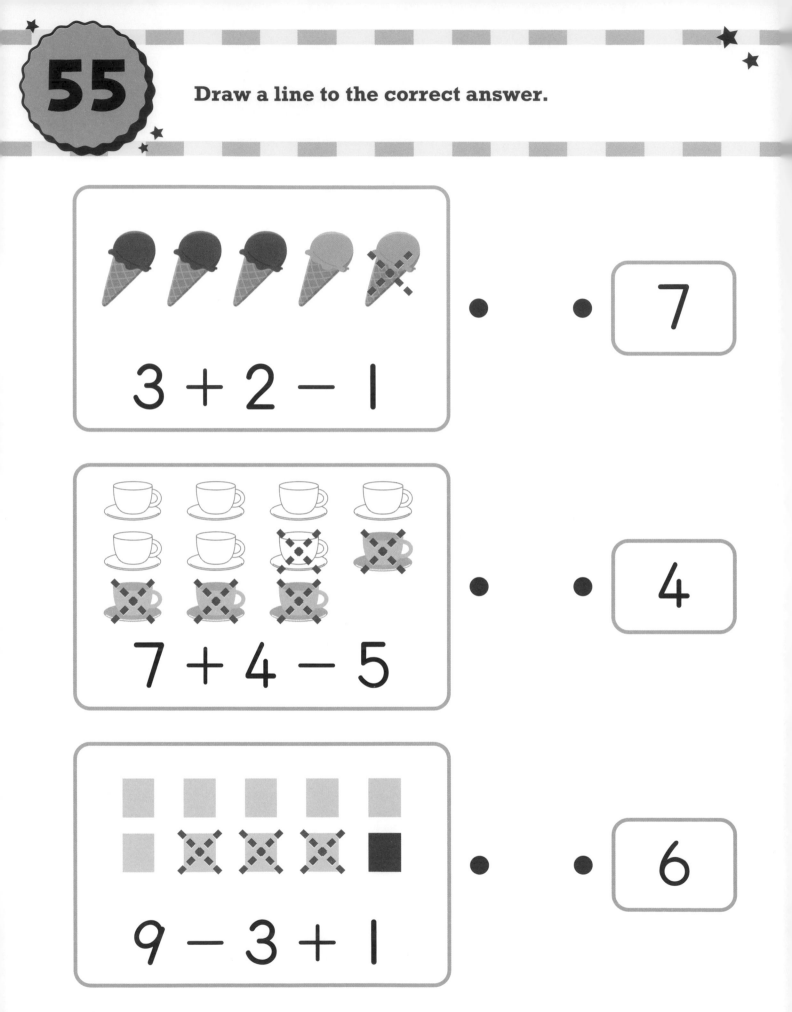

3 + 2 − 1

7

7 + 4 − 5

4

9 − 3 + 1

6

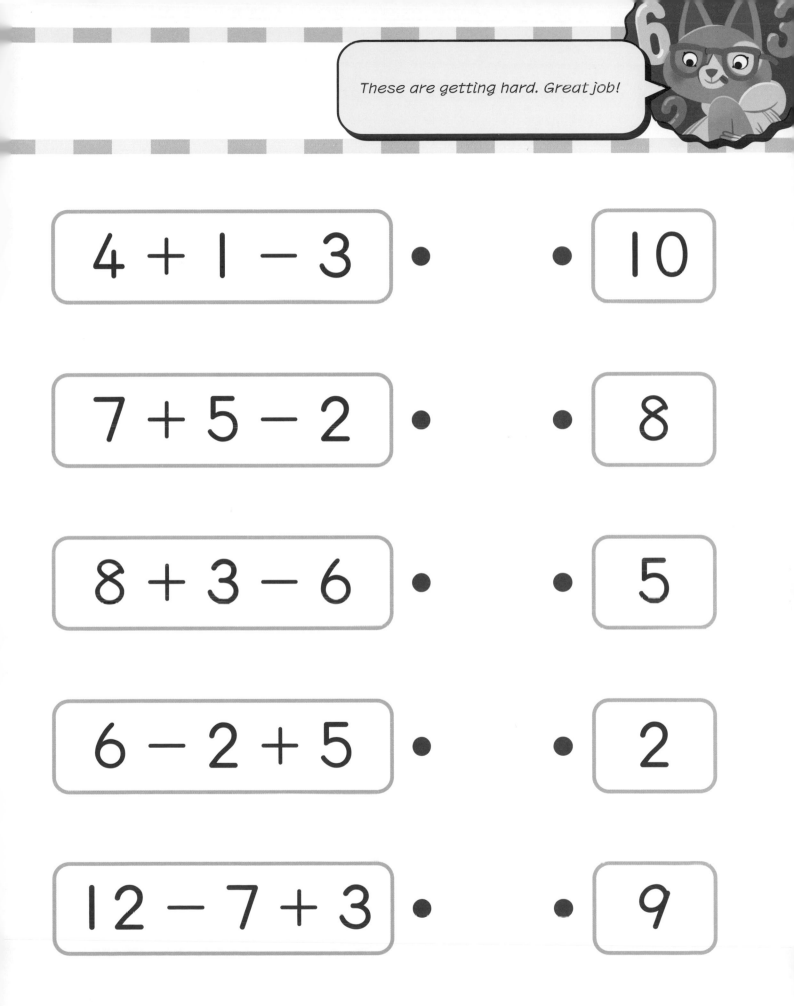

4 + 1 − 3 • • 10

7 + 5 − 2 • • 8

8 + 3 − 6 • • 5

6 − 2 + 5 • • 2

12 − 7 + 3 • • 9

Draw a line to the correct answer.

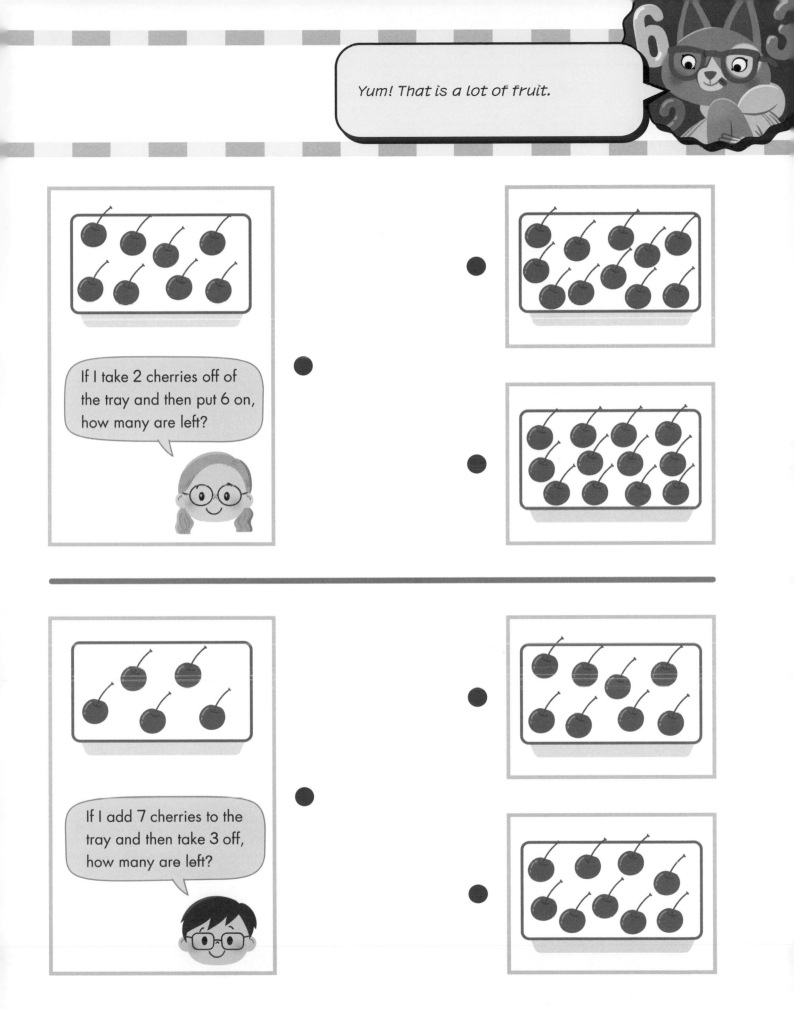

Place a check mark (✔) for correct statements and an "✗" for incorrect statements.

The number of sea turtles and jellyfish combined is 2 more than the number of shells.

The number of sea turtles and shells combined is 2 more than the number of yellow fish.

The number of jellyfish and shells combined is 3 more than the number of yellow fish.

The number of shells and yellow fish combined is 3 more than the number of red fish.

Answer Key

Everyday Math *Addition & Subtraction*

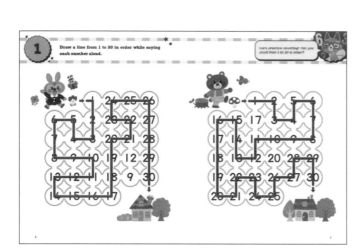

pages 4–5

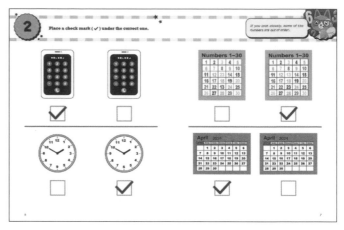

pages 6–7

pages 8–9

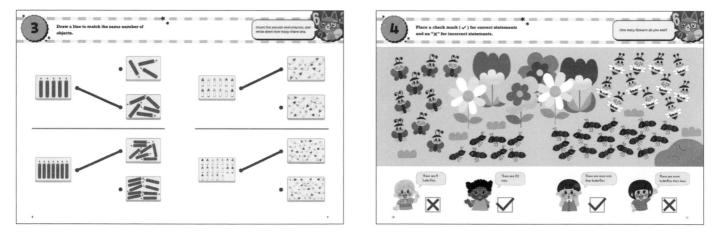

pages 10–11

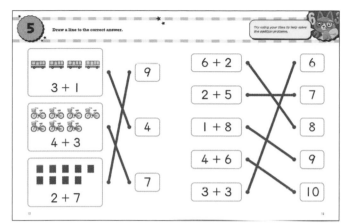

pages 12–13

pages 14–15

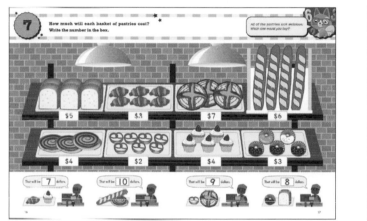

pages 16–17

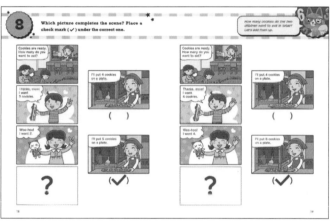

pages 18–19

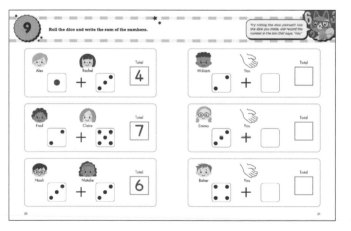

pages 20–21

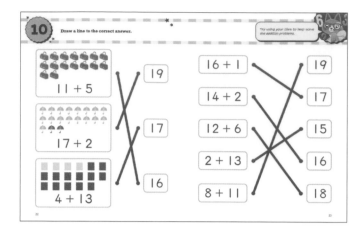

pages 22–23

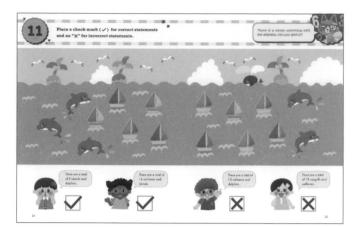

pages 24–25

pages 26–27

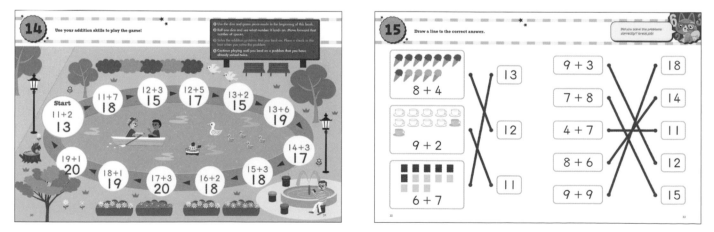

pages 28–29

pages 30–31

pages 32–33

pages 34–35

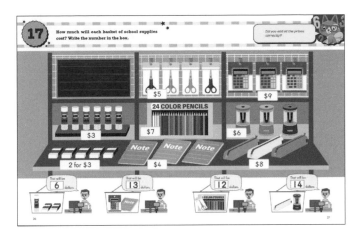

pages 36–37

pages 38–39

pages 40–41

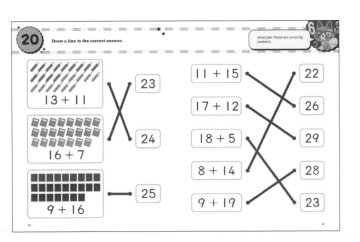

pages 42–43

pages 44–45

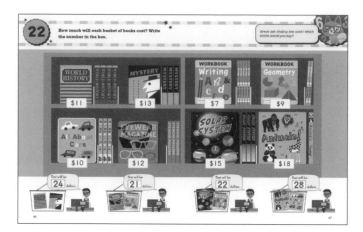

pages 46–47

pages 48–49

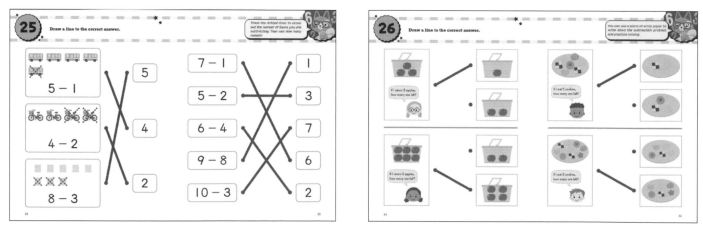

pages 50–51

pages 52–53

pages 54–55

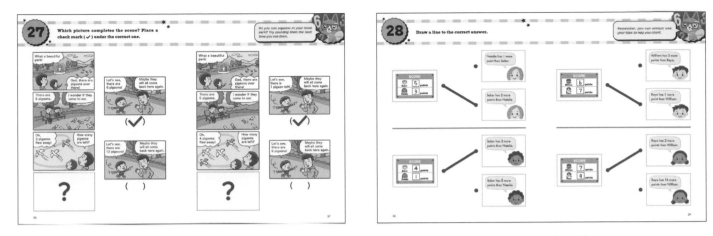

pages 56–57

pages 58–59

pages 60–61

pages 62–63

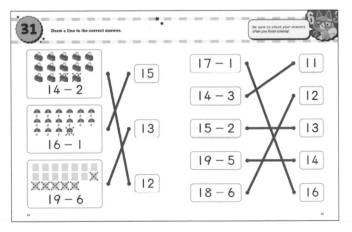

pages 64–65

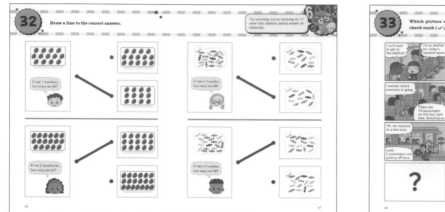

pages 66–67

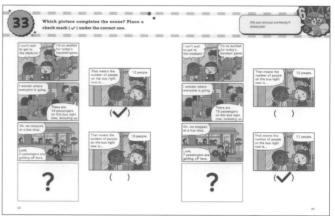

pages 68–69

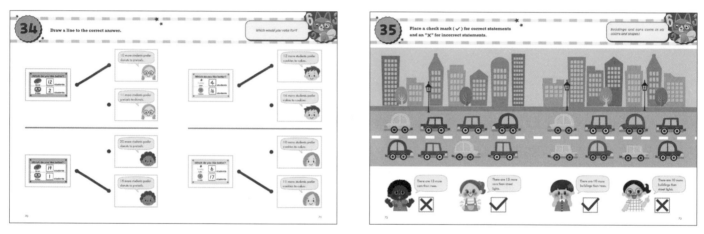

pages 70–71

pages 72–73

pages 74–75

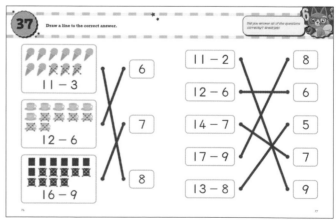

pages 76–77

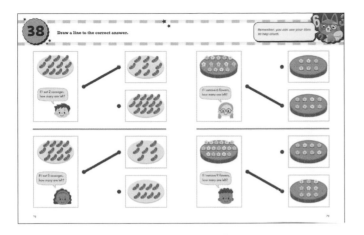

pages 78–79

pages 80–81

pages 82–83

pages 84–85

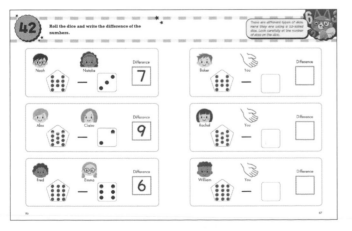

pages 86–87

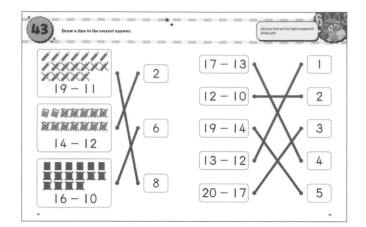

pages 88–89

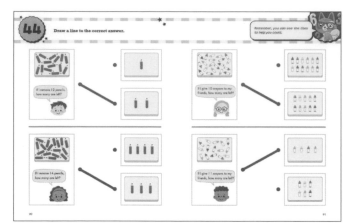

pages 90–91

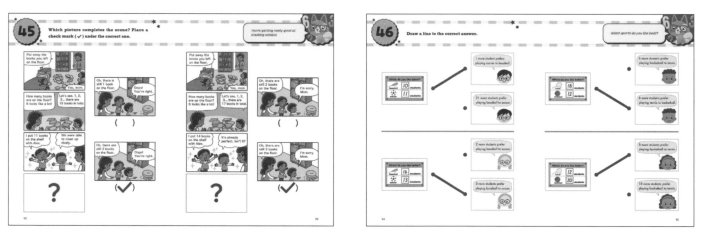

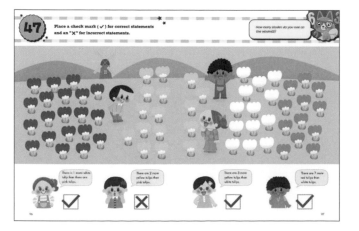

pages 92–93

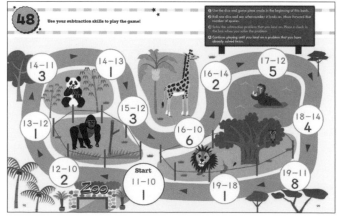

pages 94–95

pages 96–97

pages 98–99

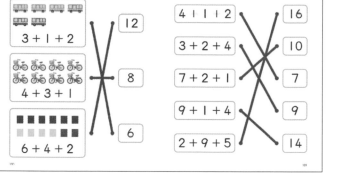

pages 100–101

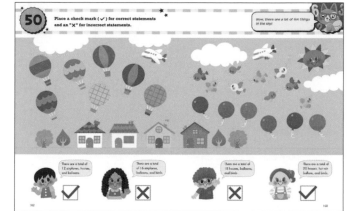

pages 102–103

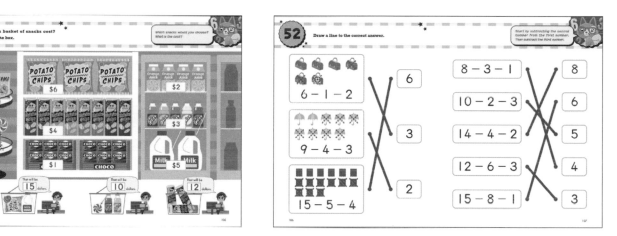

pages 104–105

pages 106–107

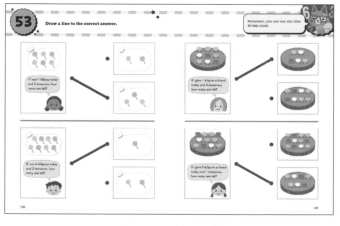

pages 108–109

pages 110–111

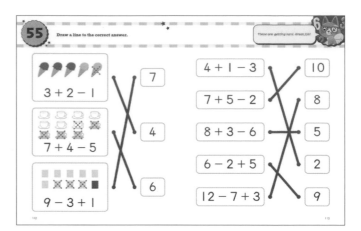

pages 112–113

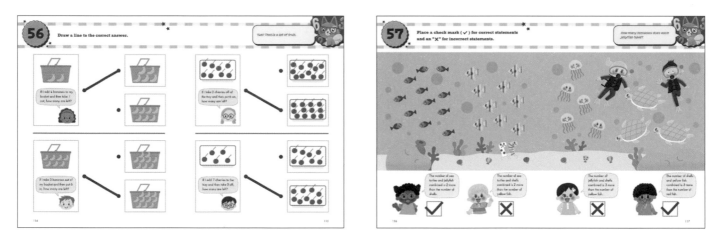

pages 114–115

pages 116–117